ROUTLEDGE LIBRARY EDITIONS:
FAMILY

I0127896

Volume 18

FAMILY AND
KINSHIP IN
MODERN BRITAIN

FAMILY AND KINSHIP IN MODERN BRITAIN

CHRISTOPHER TURNER

Routledge
Taylor & Francis Group

LONDON AND NEW YORK

First published in 1969 by Routledge & Kegan Paul Ltd

This edition first published in 2023
by Routledge
4 Park Square, Milton Park, Abingdon, Oxon OX14 4RN

and by Routledge
605 Third Avenue, New York, NY 10158

Routledge is an imprint of the Taylor & Francis Group, an informa business

British Library Cataloguing in Publication Data
A catalogue record for this book is available from the British Library

ISBN: 978-1-032-51072-9 (Set)
ISBN: 978-1-032-53698-9 (Volume 18) (hbk)
ISBN: 978-1-032-53705-4 (Volume 18) (pbk)
ISBN: 978-1-003-41323-3 (Volume 18) (ebk)

DOI: 10.4324/9781003413233

Publisher's Note
The publisher has gone to great lengths to ensure the quality of this reprint but points out that some imperfections in the original copies may be apparent.

Disclaimer
The publisher has made every effort to trace copyright holders and would welcome correspondence from those they have been unable to trace.

Family and Kinship in Modern Britain

An introduction

by Christopher Turner
Lecturer in Sociology, School of Social Studies
University of East Anglia

LONDON
ROUTLEDGE & KEGAN PAUL
NEW YORK: HUMANITIES PRESS

First published 1969
by Routledge & Kegan Paul Ltd
Broadway House, 68-74 Carter Lane
London, E.C.4
Printed in Great Britain
by Northumberland Press Limited
Gateshead
SBN 7100 6345 8 (C)
SBN 7100 6347 4 (P)

General editor's introduction

Today Sociology is going through a phase of great expansion. Not only is there a widespread general interest in the subject, but there is a rapid growth in the number of new courses at Universities, Colleges of Education, and elsewhere. As a result there is an increasing number of potential readers of introductory textbooks. Some will be motivated by general interest; some will want to find out enough about the subject to see whether they would like to pursue a formal course in it; and others will already be following courses into which an element of Sociology has been fused. One approach to these readers is by means of the comprehensive introductory volume giving a general coverage of the field of sociology; another is by means of a series of monographs each providing an introduction to a selected topic. Both these approaches have their advantages and disadvantages. The *Library of Sociology* adopts the second approach. It will cover a more extensive range of topics than could be dealt with in a single volume; while at the same time each volume will provide a thorough introductory treatment of any one topic. The reader who has little or no knowledge in the field will find within any particular book a foundation upon which to build, and to extend by means of the suggestions for further reading.

Both common experience and the writings of social scientists agree in assigning great importance to the family. In the words of a well-known textbook of Sociology, 'the family is by far the most important primary group in Society'. Why should this be? There are several reasons. First, in tracing out the different ways in which a biological relationship is built upon and modified in different societies insight into the great variability of social structures may be obtained. Second, the family is an important sociological unit since through it a variety of functions are mediated, among them the provision of food, shelter, and protection, especially for the young, and especially in other systems than our own it has economic functions as well. Third, and perhaps most important, it is the environment within which children are socialised to the social patterns which make up the society they have newly entered. The primary concern of the sociologist is to understand the functioning of the family in any given society and to set these observations in the more general framework of the relation of kinship systems to social structures.

These are very general questions and in this book Dr. Turner's aims are more limited. His objective is to present a conceptual scheme for the analysis of family and kinship in modern Britain. However, in doing so he uses the particular example to illustrate general principles of the analysis of kinship. But the family is not a static entity and the author's approach to his subject is processual. There are two aspects to this. In the first place, any individual family may be seen as passing through a cycle of development and decline, this Dr. Turner calls 'the developmental cycle'. In the second place, the family is an element in social structure and as the structure changes so does the family. Hence selected illustrations of the relationship between family, kinship and the wider social structure are considered.

The study of the family, then, is inexorably linked with other aspects of the study of sociology; with class, education, socialisation, occupation and many other topics which will be found in accompanying volumes.

A. R. EMERSON

Contents

CONTENTS

Tables and Charts

1
Family and kinship: a sociological perspective

Introduction

The major task of sociologists working in the field of kinship and marriage is to develop theories which lead to an understanding of the structure and operation of kinship systems, and to examine the relationships between kinship systems and other aspects of social structure. It is obviously important that the concepts in kinship theory should be closely related to empirical material which is drawn from societies throughout the world. The literature on the kinship systems of differing societies contains a wealth of information, though by no means a complete catalogue of what the sociologist would like to know. Unfortunately there is no unified body of theory which helps to bring this material together at the present time. At best there is agreement on a few fundamental concepts and structural principles which provide a common framework for the analysis of kinship systems.

Ideally the sociologist aims to study kinship and marriage in both historical and comparative perspective. In this text the major focus of attention is upon the system of kinship and marriage which exists in contemporary Britain. Nevertheless, in order to adopt a sociological approach to the data, an introduction to certain basic concepts is necessary. The concepts selected for examination are social position, social relationship, social activity, social descent, marriage, nuclear family, and domestic group. The first three concepts, social position, social relationship, and social activity, are general concepts used in sociological analysis. The others, social descent, marriage, nuclear family and domestic group, are key concepts for the comparative analysis of kinship systems. These particular concepts have been selected because they are highly relevant to the analysis of the British kinship system, but an attempt has been made to introduce them in a more general perspective. It is hoped that this will give the reader some insight into how the British kinship system varies from certain other systems. The ideas upon which this text is based are drawn from a wide variety of sources. For the benefit of the reader who wishes to pursue major theoretical points and to read some of the basic empirical material, selected references are included in the text.

Social position, social relationship and social activity

The three concepts of social position, social relationship and social activity are closely interrelated. It is possible to give formal definitions, but a concrete example is perhaps a more instructive starting point. Two social positions which are recognised by sociologists and non-sociologists alike are the positions of husband and wife. These are complementary positions, and the relationship between them may be viewed in terms of the social activities relevant to that relationship. In general, given two or more identifiable positions, it is possible to examine each pair of positions to see whether there is a social relationship involved, and, if so, to see what social activities are involved in the relationship. This is the approach adopted in the present text, though it should be noted that alternative approaches are equally viable, but usually more complex.

The sociologist attempts to analyse social positions and social relationships independently of the particular individuals involved in them at a given point in time. It is by some such process of abstraction from 'the real world' that he begins to build up theoretical models of social structure. The primary focus of attention is upon enduring or recurrent characteristics of social positions and social relationships, and upon the social activities which are associated with them. It is no less important, however, to consider the processes by which social structures are perpetuated and changed through time. It is on the basis of such detailed and systematic analysis that the sociologist attempts to determine the extent to which human behaviour can be predicted from a knowledge of the structure and operation of societies.

The range of social positions under consideration in the present text has been limited by the decision to focus upon kinship and marriage. Kinship positions are organised into systems of kin relationships according to two main principles, (i) The tracing of social descent, and (ii) the social recognition of marriage ties. These two principles are found in every society, but operate in highly complex combinations to give rise to a wide range of differing kinship structures. Before considering either of these principles, however, it is important to emphasise that the kinship theorist is concerned with socially recognised rela-

3

tionships which are expressed in terms of marriage and/or descent. Kin relationships do not necessarily coincide with biological or genetic relationships. The Trobrianders of North West Melanesia for example, fail to acknowledge the fact of biological paternity, but nevertheless recognise the father-son relationship in their kinship reckoning (Malinowski, 1932). Legal adoption in Britain provides a further example: there is usually no genetic link between parents and an adopted child, but a socially sanctioned kin relationship exists.

Social descent and marriage

The principles of social descent and marriage are each vital to an understanding of the other. The key relationships are those between husband and wife, and between parent and child. Marriage involves the establishment of a husband-wife relationship on the basis of which socially recognised joint parenthood becomes possible. Social descent rests upon a socially recognised relationship between parent and child, which may exist independently of marriage in specific instances, but which commonly implies marriage between parents.

A basic distinction is usually made between monogamous and polygamous systems of marriage. In the former, the general principle of marriage is that each husband may have only one wife, and conversely each wife may have only one husband at a time. Serial monogamy is often permitted, i.e. re-marriage may follow the dissolution of a previous union. The British system of marriage affords a good example of this type. Polygamy takes one of two major forms, either polygyny or polyandry, though there are many different permutations of

4

each of these types. According to the polygynous principle each husband may take more than one wife at a time. This is the more widespread form of polygamy and is fairly common throughout Africa and the Middle East. *Kinship and Marriage among the Nuer* contains a particularly well documented analysis of one form of polygynous system (Evans-Pritchard, 1951). Polyandry is the complementary type of system to polygyny. Each wife is permitted to take one or more husbands. The Todas of India provide a good example of one form of polyandry (Rivers, 1906).

In distinguishing between monogamous and polygamous systems of marriage it should be noted that the monogamous principle prohibits a polygamous type of union, but the converse is not true. In fact, available evidence suggests that where the polygamous principle is in operation, unions approximating to the monogamous type are common, and indeed sometimes predominate.

The tracing of social descent from child to parent in each ascending generation is a basic principle of all kinship systems. Such direct kin ties may be reckoned through either the mother or the father, or through both. A convention normally adopted when analysing social descent is to use the term 'ego' to denote the position from which descent is being examined. This helps to avoid terminological confusion, as it gives a fixed point of reference from which relationships are traced. A distinction is usually drawn between multilineal and unilineal principles of descent. In a multilineal system, descent is traced through both male and female lines in each ascending generation from ego. In unilineal systems it is traced primarily through either the male or the female line. When descent is traced primarily through the male line the system is

5

designated patrilineal, when it is traced primarily through the female line the system is designated matrilineal.

The existence of a multilineal system does not necessarily imply that descent must be traced through all possible direct lines, and the term *selective multilineal descent system* provides a more accurate description of structures of this type. The British kinship system furnishes a good example of one form of selective multilineal system. No one line is necessarily emphasised to the exclusion of others, but the male line receives a special emphasis in that the wife customarily takes her husband's surname, and it is subsequently transmitted to both sons and daughters. The transmission of hereditary titles also tends to be biased in favour of the male line. In other words certain direct descent links tend to be emphasised at the expense of others, because of the rights, obligations and expectations associated with them.

So-called unilineal descent systems are in fact a very special form of selective multilineal descent system. In unilineal systems, either patrilineal or matrilineal descent provides a basic organising principle in society. The ideology of patrilineal or matrilineal descent is closely linked with the exercise of social power. This power may take a wide variety of concrete forms, e.g. administrative power, power over property, and/or power over the sacred, to name only the three most salient forms. The precise forms of social power connected with any particular unilineal descent system is a matter for empirical investigation. The term unilineal descent is used because of the importance of *the social rights and obligations* which correlate with the patrilineal or matrilineal tracing of descent, not because unilineal kin ties are the only descent ties which are socially recognised. Examples of both patrilineal and matrilineal descent systems may be found in *African systems of Kinship and Marriage* (Radcliffe-Brown & Forde, 1950).

The relationship between full siblings (i.e. the children of the same two parents) is of special interest. In terms of social descent it can be construed as a relationship in which shared descent from the same mother and/or the same father provides the crucial link. In terms of marriage it can be construed as a relationship between two offspring of the same marriage. These two expressions of the same relationship may be complementary, but the relationship is generally phrased in terms of descent ideology by participants in a kinship system, and analysed by sociologists in terms of descent theory.

It is possible for systems of kin relationships to be traced in terms of (i) complex sets of parent-child linkages, and (ii) affinal ties. It is usual, however, for intersibling relationships to be used alongside parent-child and affinal relationships, both in kinship reckoning and in the analysis of kinship structures. This convention has been adopted for the present text. Allowing for sex differences, eight basic social positions are involved in kinship reckoning: those of father, mother, son, daughter, brother, sister, husband and wife. It is possible to make further distinctions according to the orders of seniority both siblings and of spouses. Nevertheless, these are the basic social positions through which kin relationships are traced, and in terms of which genealogies can be most precisely expressed. The actual range of kin relationships traced through social descent and affinity varies considerably both between kinship systems and also within each particular system. This is a matter which is perhaps best left open for empirical investigation.

Nuclear families and domestic groups

The term 'family' is subject to so many different usages that sociologists have found it necessary to develop a more precise terminology. The *nuclear family* is the unit consisting of one husband (father), one wife (mother) and their sons and/or daughters, if any (brothers and sisters). The relationships involved are those basic to kinship reckoning: husband-wife, parent-child and inter-sibling relationships. (The terms elementary family, immediate family and conjugal family are also used to refer to this same constellation of social positions, but with varying nuances of meaning.)

The set of social positions and social relationships which makes up the nuclear family is common to every society, but the nuclear family is by no means a significant social unit in every society. The factors of critical importance are firstly the way in which nuclear family roles are enmeshed into the wider kinship structure, and secondly the way in which domestic activities are organised. In Britain the nuclear family occupies a dominant structural position, and relationships between nuclear family members tend to be of much greater social significance than other kinship links. The British kinship system is often described as a 'conjugal family system' precisely because of the centrality of the nuclear (or conjugal) family. Certain other kinship systems, however, differ markedly.

With polygamous systems of marriage it is useful to distinguish between the nuclear family and the compound family. The polygynous compound family consists of a husband, each of his wives and such children as they have between them. The polyandrous compound family consists of a wife, each of her husbands and all their children. In this way, analytically distinguishable nuclear family units are combined into a wider social unit. In a compound family each analytically distinguishable nuclear family unit may either be of considerable social significance, or alternatively may not even be socially recognised.

A much larger kin unit, commonly though not invariably associated with a unilineal descent ideology, is the corporate descent group. This consists of a group of kin who are united by their collective responsibility for decision-making, in respect of jural, administrative or ceremonial activities. Decision-making, in this context, is almost invariably the province of males, and it is usual for claims to descent from a common ancestor (either male or female) to be a major criterion for membership in the male decision-making group. Where units of this type exist, they are likely to impose limitations on the freedom of decision-making of any smaller kin group, such as a compound or nuclear family.

The concept 'domestic group' is difficult to define with any precision. It is essential to realise that the organisation of domestic activities does not necessarily focus upon *one* domestic unit which emerges in all situations (see Goody, 1958, pp. 53-56). Moreover activities which are regarded as falling within the sphere of domestic organisation vary from society to society. Thus each nuclear or compound family may at some time form a domestic group for some purposes, but does not invariably do so.

Among the polygynous LoDagaba, for example, Goody distinguishes at least three major units which comprise domestic groups. Firstly there is the basic co-operative farming unit which consists of a married man and all his sons, or of a set of full brothers, who are aided to some extent by their wives and young children. In contrast, the

9

domestic group primarily concerned with distribution, preparation and consumption of produce consists of a married woman, her unmarried children and her husband. Since the LoDagaba are polygynous this means that a husband may belong to more than one domestic group of this second type. The third type of domestic group is a dwelling unit, the occupants of one homestead. The composition of each of these domestic groups changes through time, and recurrent patterns of change have given rise to the important concept of *The Development Cycle of Domestic Groups* (Goody, 1958).

In any society the organisation and composition of domestic groups can be subjected to empirical investigation at any given point in time. Certain domestic groups may comprise all or only some members of a nuclear or compound family, and in some instances other relatives or unrelated persons may supplement the central family core. There may also be non-familial domestic groups in a society. The changing composition of domestic groups can also be charted through time, and empirically demonstrated. The processes of fission and fusion by which domestic groups are formed, increased, renewed, dissolved and replaced can be subjected to systematic analysis. One of the most important aspects of the study of kinship systems is that concerned with the extent to which kin relationships and the processes of marriage and family development can be understood in terms of the development cycle of domestic groups.

Examples of several forms of domestic group can be found in Britain, but one particular type of domestic group, the household, is pre-eminent. A *household* may be defined as a unit composed of persons who both share a common residence, and regularly eat together. The majority of households in contemporary Britain are composed of a nuclear family or partial nuclear family unit. It is necessary for analytical purposes, however, to distinguish between the nuclear family and the household. A particular nuclear family unit continues in existence as long as its members maintain their social relationships, regardless of whether they continue to live and eat together. The household, in contrast, is a social unit based upon shared domestic activities, and membership is not necessarily based upon any kinship criterion.

Summary and discussion

The main purpose of this chapter has been to highlight some of the major characteristics of different types of kinship systems. No attempt has been made to elaborate on the subtleties and complexities of any one kinship system, nor to distinguish between the variety of differing forms which could be classified under any one of the general headings such as monogamy, matrilineal descent, or domestic groups. Any of these tasks would merit a substantial text in its own right. Nevertheless the brief outline presented should make it clear that the British system of kinship and marriage, is but one of many possible alternatives. It should be equally evident that an assumption that any particular kinship system is the 'natural one' and that the remainder constitute either deviations, or imperfectly developed systems is totally untenable from the sociological viewpoint.

Against the background of comparative studies of family and kinship systems throughout the world, the primary aim of this text is to introduce the student to the monogamous, selective multi-lineal, conjugal family system of contemporary Britain. An attempt is made to provide partial answers at least to the following sociologically significant questions.

1. How do the rules of descent and affinity operate in the British kinship system?

2. How is the nuclear family integrated into British kinship structure?

3. How is the nuclear family related to the household in Britain?

4. In what way are an individual's family and kinship roles interconnected with his other social roles?

5. How does the family and kinship system fit into the general institutional framework of contemporary British society?

6. What evidence is available to indicate systematic trends of change in the British system?

Underpinning these, there are always the basic questions of sociological research. How adequate is the empirical material, and where is further research most needed?

2
The British kinship system

Each individual comes to the study of family and kinship with some general experience and common sense ideas about his or her own kinship system. Parsons writing on the kinship system of the United States, emphasised the similar starting point of the sociologist 'To a considerable extent the material must come from the kind of common sense and general experience which have been widely held to be of dubious scientific standing' (Parsons, 1954, p. 117). Since 1943, when Parsons first published his analysis, a considerable volume of research on kinship has been undertaken throughout the world. Parsons' original insights and interpretations have proved a useful starting point, especially for the study of kinship in the context of modern industrial societies, but there have clearly been many theoretical and empirical research contributions since then. In the present text, an attempt is made to outline a framework for the analysis of British kinship behaviour, which, it is hoped, will present new and different ways of thinking about family and kinship to those readers making their first venture into the field of sociology.

Modern Britain as previously emphasised is character-ised by a conjugal family system. The central kin grouping is the monogamous nuclear family. The significance of the term 'conjugal family system' is further highlighted when the kinship system is viewed as a series of interlocking nuclear families. With very few exceptions, every indi-vidual is expected to belong to two nuclear family units during his or her lifetime. The first of these, the family into which a person is born, is called the 'family of origin': the second is formed by an individual's marriage, and is distinguished as the 'family of marriage' (see Appendix). A family of origin and family of marriage cannot share more than one common member unless marriage rules are broken, since an individual is forbidden to marry a mem-ber of his or her family of origin. Each nuclear family unit may be regarded as a family of marriage from the parents' point of view, and as a family of origin for their children at one and the same time.

The current kinship terminology provides one starting point from which to build up a picture of the reckoning of kin relationships beyond the boundaries of the nuclear family. Each individual has a unique configuration of actual kin, but the same terminology suffices to describe each ego-centred network of kin. British kinship termin-ology does not indicate precise genealogical relationships, except within the nuclear family. It serves to delineate general categories of kin, who are related to ego in terms of social descent or marriage. Ego's grandfather for example, may be either the mother's father or the father's father, and ego's brother-in-law may be either the hus-band of any one of ego's sisters, or a brother of ego's spouse.

It is useful to distinguish between certain categories of

kin within ego's total kin network. One important distinction is that between relatives reckoned by social descent and relatives by marriage. The former category can be termed ego's *kindred*, the latter ego's *affines*. Within each of these categories it is possible to make further analytical distinctions.

Kindred

Social descent is reckoned predominantly in terms of a 'blood' or genetic relationship in Britain, and it is necessary to note that consanguinity provides an extremely important underpinning for the tracing of social descent. A special, almost mystical, significance is attached to the blood tie, illustrated in such sayings as 'blood is thicker than water'. The differentiation of legitimate from illegitimate births suggests clearly that the blood tie is not of over-riding importance *per se*. The term 'consanguinity' attains additional significance when it is used to describe a relationship which has both genetic and social aspects. Adoption provides a somewhat uneasy means for grafting an individual into a prevailing system of consanguineous relationships. Upon adoption, the adoptee, in theory at least, obtains a new kindred.

Within ego's kindred a general distinction can be made between individuals who stand in the direct line of descent and those who do not. Within the direct line of descent, ego's *descendants* (children, children's children, and so on in each descending generation) can be distinguished from ego's *forbears* (parents, grandparents, great-grandparents and so on in each ascending generation). The number of descendants is determined by the vicissitudes of biological reproduction and adoption, and is thus subject to considerable variation. The number of forbears can theoretically double in each generation (two parents, four grandparents, eight great-grandparents, etc.), but marriage between kin in any ascending generation will reduce the overall number of forbears. This holds true even if the kin relationship involved is extremely distant and not known by the parties to the marriage. Members of ego's kindred who are not in ego's direct line of descent share at least one common forbear with ego, i.e. the two kinsmen are both descendants of this particular forbear.

It is evident that ego's kindred at a particular point in time, including both the dead and the living must, for practical reasons, be limited in some way. Yet there are no fixed rules for determining such limits in the British kinship system. In fact, the variability and optional nature of kin recognition is a major characteristic of the system. Nevertheless it is useful to make certain analytical distinctions in terms of degrees of relationship within the kindred.

Each member of ego's family of origin is related to him or her by ties of consanguinity or adoption: so are members of ego's family of marriage with the single exception of the spouse. This group of consanguineous or adoptive kin—ego's, mother, father, brother(s), sister(s), son(s), and daughter(s)—can be usefully distinguished as ego's relatives 'in the first degree' (see Appendix). In the British kinship system there is an expectation that each member of this group will at some time in the life cycle share the same home as ego. Thus social relationships are expected to be established on the basis of first degree relationships.

Second degree relatives may be characterised as kindred, who currently belong, or have belonged, to the same nuclear family as one of ego's first degree relations. Each of ego's first degree kin can link ego with only one further nuclear family unit. These are the families of origin of ego's mother and father, and the families of marriage, if and when established, of ego's siblings and children. Ego's second degree relatives thus include four grandparents, and a variable number of uncles and aunts (i.e. ego's parents' siblings), of nephews and nieces (i.e. ego's siblings' children) and of ego's own grandchildren (see Appendix). It is interesting to note that this is the stage at which terminological distinctions between maternal and paternal kin are dropped.

First cousins are here excluded from the group of second degree kin on the grounds that they belong, not to the families of origin of uncles or aunts, but to their families of marriage. This is consistent with the rules of inter-marriage, which forbid marriage with consanguineous kin of first or second degree, as defined here. Nevertheless it is not uncommon for first cousins to be included as second degree or 'close' kin (e.g. Rees, 1950, p. 74). It is theoreti-cally possible to extend the chain of family linkages to a further circle of kin through second degree relatives, and to continue adding successive circles in this manner. At the present time, however, it seems more useful to group together all consanguineous kin, beyond the first and sec-ond degree, as 'peripheral relations'.

Little attention has been specifically devoted to the study of second degree or peripheral kin. Rees (1950) observed that more than three-quarters of the families in Llanfihangel were related to at least one other family, by kinship within the second degree (Rees includes first cousins in this calculation). One third of the families, more-over, were linked to between five and twelve other families within this same degree. Llanfihangel, however, has a very closely knit kinship structure, and is certainly not typical of the country as a whole. In fact, it is one of the most kin-centred rural communities which has yet been studied in Britain. Even so we are left to guess at the frequency of interaction between second degree kin living within the community, though from the evidence presented it is fairly clear that the quality of the relationship is expected to be characteristically close and friendly.

A study of kin relationships in two districts of Oxford reported: 'Typically, it would seem, these English urban families pay little attention to blood relatives, even to those as close as first cousins' (Mogey, 1956, p. 78). The evidence in *Tradition and Change: A Study of Banbury* (Stacey, 1960), and *Coal is Our Life* (Dennis, Henriques, and Slaughter, 1956), would support similar conclusions for other urban working class areas. Mogey was, implicitly at least, comparing the situation of urban Oxford with that of rural Ireland, where he had previously carried out a study (Mogey, 1947). Both peripheral and second degree kin also appear to play a somewhat more important part in the rural communities of 'Pentrediwaith' (Frankenberg, 1957), Gosforth (Williams, 1956) and 'Ashworthy' (Williams, 1963). Thus there seems to be a fairly clear cut rural-urban contrast in this respect.

The paucity of information on relationships with second degree or peripheral kin is, in part, a result of the lack of systematic investigation, and in part a reflection of the way in which the British kinship system operates. The permissiveness allowed in establishing social relationships with kin, and the openness of a multi-lineal system means that an individual may choose whether or not to recognise more distant kin, and has a further choice concerning whether or not to establish social relationships on the basis of known kinship links. Generally speaking an individual actually recognises first and second degree relations, and maintains some form of social contact with first degree kin, and with second degree relatives in the direct line of descent. Knowledge of or contact with peripheral kin is extremely variable.

Affines

The distinction between kindred and affines is usually considered basic to an understanding of the British kinship system. Most studies emphasise the importance of kindred. Williams, for example, makes only brief references to affines, in his chapter on kinship, but notes that '. . . ties by marriage are the basis for social relationships and in some cases these ties are closer than those existing between individuals and their remote kindred' (1956, p. 74). It is impossible, however, to analyse relationships within the kindred to the exclusion of affines. It is convenient to use the idea of an ego-centred network of affines as an analytic tool, in much the same way as it was convenient to conceptualise the kindred as an ego-centred network of consanguineous and adopted kin. Upon marriage the kindred of each spouse becomes a network of *direct affines* of the other spouse, and members of both of these networks are potential kindred of children born of the marriage. Ego's network of affines also contains *indirect affines*. These can be conveniently divided into two main categories; firstly there are the spouses of members of ego's kindred, and secondly spouses of ego's direct affines. These indirect affines do not become consanguineous kin of ego's children, although their offspring do, since the indirect affine is married to one of ego's kindred or direct affines.

This leaves the residual problem of whether there are any other categories of affines which should be recognised for purposes of sociological analysis. The sociologist could, for example, consider the direct affines of each of ego's descendants, not just the descendants' spouses, as affines. Similarly, the kindred of each of ego's indirect affines, excluding their descendants, could be categorised as affines. Further, but more remote categories of affines could be built up using similar principles. For purposes of the present text any affines belonging to such categories will be labelled '*quasi-affines*'. The relevance of these arbitrarily defined '*quasi-affines*' to the study of the British kinship system is difficult to evaluate. It is perhaps worth noting, however, that the ramifications of marriage alliances are potentially much more complex than those of social descent, if 'quasi-affines' are included in kinship analysis.

Research has been carried out in Swansea relevant to a discussion of networks of affines. It was found that affines of a parent's siblings were not clearly distinguished from consanguineous kin, and the term 'merged affines', was adopted to describe such persons (Rosser and Harris, 1961). The common use of the kin terms 'aunt' and 'uncle' to refer both to ego's parents' siblings and to their respective spouses, is clearly one factor which makes such merging possible. On the other hand, there is no evidence to show how widespread this merging of affines is. In the Pennine parish which I studied, people went out of their way to disclaim kinship with their parents' siblings' spouses. Common responses were 'He's no kin of mine, he belongs to . . .', or 'We call her auntie, but really she's no kin'. It should be noted, however, that this does not absolve the sociologist from treating such persons within an analytical framework of kinship, but merely makes his task more difficult. As Rosser and Harris point out, this area of the British kinship system has been widely ignored, and a considerable amount of further research is required. An associated problem is that of the extension of kinship terms to unrelated persons. This is perhaps most common in the case of close friends of ego's parents, who are addressed as 'aunt' or 'uncle' by ego. This again is an area in which little systematic information has been collected, but would fit in well with research on merged affines.

Following the pattern set in distinguishing between first degree kindred, second degree kindred and distant or peripheral kindred, it is possible to distinguish first degree affines, second degree affines and other affines. All first degree affines are direct affines (ego's spouse and first degree kindred of ego's spouse). Second degree affines fall into two categories direct (second degree kindred of spouse) and indirect (spouses of ego's siblings and spouses of ego's spouses siblings) (see Appendix). Other affines can also be divided into direct and indirect. Rosser and Harris illustrate quite clearly that both first and second degree affines (whom they group together as primary affines) are normally integrated into the kinship network of ego's family of marriage, at least in Swansea, and they emphasise the selectivity which leads to the inclusion of only a few of the possible secondary affines. In addition, after careful consideration of the evidence, they come to the conclusion that the husband tends to strike a rough balance in maintaining social relationships with his own blood kin and those of his wife, whereas the wife shows a small but consistent bias towards maintaining more relationships with her own blood kin.

The kinship universe

The term *kinship universe* is used to denote all the kindred and affines of all related members of a household (following Firth, 1956). The usefulness of the concept is well illustrated by a brief consideration of the major principles underlying the development of the respective ego-centred kin networks of three individuals, a husband, his wife and their unmarried child. The general principles underlying development of the total kin networks of each of the three individuals are the same, but it is the interplay of these principles which is both instructive and important. Each individual at birth, acquires a kindred and a set of indirect affines (i.e. spouses of members of the kindred). Subsequently additions to the kindred occur when children are born to or adopted by the individual and existing members of the kindred. New indirect affines are acquired when members of the kindred marry. Such additions to the total kin network continue throughout an individual's life. When two individuals marry, the kindred of the husband become direct affines of the wife, and conversely kindred of the wife become direct affines of the husband, but all of these persons become kindred (and not direct affines) of a child born of the marriage. Indirect affines of the husband also become indirect affines of the wife, and vice versa, and all of these become indirect affines of a child born of the marriage (i.e. spouses of members of his/her kindred). After marriage, additions to the direct affines of husband or wife occur when children are born to or adopted by existing direct affines, and the category of indirect affines of husband or wife is augmented by the marriage of direct affines, as well as by existing members of the kindred.

22

The pooled knowledge of all related members of a household about ties of social descent and affinity is required to build up a picture of the complete kin universe of the household, but the knowledge of kinship ties does not necessarily mean that social contact is maintained with all persons in the kin universe. In fact it is usual to find dead persons included as members of the kin universe. This leads directly to the question of how the size of the kin universe is kept within manageable proportions. Births, adoptions and marriages provide additions to the kin universe, but dead kinfolk are not necessarily dropped from the reckoning. In practice it appears that more distant kindred and affines reckoned as part of the kin universe of an individual's household of origin tend to disappear, together with their descendants, from the reckoning of that individual's household of marriage. Also failure to maintain social contact with known kin means that information about potential additions to the kin universe is not transmitted. These processes of limitation of the kin universe of households, both between and within generations, were clearly operative in the Pennine parish which I studied.

Firth reports that the kinship universes of twelve households in a South London Borough ranged from 37-247 related persons, with an average of 146. Comparable figures for twelve households in a West Country village, studied by Williams show a range of 0-242, and an average of 133 related persons. Both sets of figures incorporated dead kinfolk, and both include kindred and affines in unspecified proportions. A shallow intergenerational depth of genealogical reckoning was another common feature: seven generations constituted the maximum and five generations the usual span. On the other hand, ties of indirect social descent extended as far as second cousins once or twice removed. These two studies provide useful exploratory bases on which to build up a thoroughgoing knowledge of the British kinship system, particularly as they both begin to examine contacts between kin. Unfortunately, however, neither study reports in detail the kinship composition of all the kin universes, nor the frequency and nature of contacts between kin, although each study contains a detailed diagram of one kin universe (Firth, 1956, p. 47; Williams, 1963, p. 159).

The kinship universe of a household which contains only parents and their unmarried children can also be examined from an analytical point of view as an ego-centred kin network of each household member. The members of such a kin universe stand in somewhat different relationships to father, mother and children. If a household comprises any other wider set of relatives, however, the problem of quasi-affines is likely to arise, when attempts are made to translate all members of the kin universe into each ego-centred network. When a household contains unrelated persons, it is perhaps most useful to conceptualise a separate kin universe for each distinct category of unrelated persons. Nevertheless, the concept of a kin universe is extremely useful as a starting point for further analysis. A kinship universe consists of the widest range of kin known to members of a household. The universe can be charted by tapping the pooled genealogical knowledge of members of the household. A detailed knowledge of the kinship universe of a household provides an excellent background against which to examine social contact between kin, since it tends to highlight the selectivity permitted in the establishment of such relationships. The term *effective kin* can be used to describe all living members of the kin universe of a particular household, with whom social contact is maintained during a given time period. Contact in this sense may mean face to face relationships of varying degrees of intensity, or communication via telephone, letter or card.

Social contacts between kin

The charting of genealogies and an examination of kinship terminology provides a useful introduction to concepts dealing with kin relationships. In the preceding discussion of kin terms, however, a definite framework was imposed upon the genealogical distinctions in order to separate out various categories of kin. One of the basic notions underlying this framework was that the kinship system could be profitably conceptualised as a series of interlocking nuclear families. This made it possible to distinguish systematically between various 'degrees' of kin, and to make some general comments concerning the types of relationship expected between two kinfolk, standing in certain categories of relationship to each other. This highly formal analysis of the kinship structure now needs to be supplemented by a more detailed analysis of the way in which the kinship system tends to operate.

It is necessary to make a clear distinction between the nuclear family and the household unit in order to understand the dynamics of the British kinship system. It is possible for an individual to belong to two nuclear families, but usually to only one household at a time. The remainder of this chapter will be devoted primarily to an analysis of inter-family contacts between families of marriage and families of origin, insofar as they constitute separate household units. The relationship between the development cycle of the family and the development cycle of the household will be discussed more fully in subsequent chapters.

Upon the establishment of a family of marriage as a household unit, both husband and wife provide a critical pivotal link with their respective families of origin. If the husband or wife is either unable or unwilling to maintain close social contact with his or her parental household, the links between the two domestic groups tend to be minimised. On the other hand, if the husband or wife maintains close contact, then all members of the two households tend to become involved. Several empirical studies emphasise the dominance of the family of origin-family of marriage linkage in extra-household kin relationships. The available evidence is fragmentary but worth reviewing.

Young and Willmott (1957) explored the connections between families of origin and families of marriage in their study of Bethnal Green, a working class area of London. The mother-daughter relationship provided the commonest axis upon which inter-family contacts were based—47% of the 133 married women in the Bethnal Green sample whose mothers were still alive but not living with them, had seen their own mothers in the 24 hours prior to the research interview. In contrast only 26% of the married men had seen their 'mums'. Comparable proportions for contact with 'mums' in the week prior to the research interview were 78% for women and 64% for men. The inter-household rather than merely the interpersonal nature of the contact is demonstrated by the figures for frequency of contact with mother-in-law. Men quite clearly tended to be drawn into the social orbit of their wives' families—66% of the husbands had seen their wives' mothers in the week prior to the research interview.

Only 53% of the wives in a comparable situation had seen their husbands' mothers.

Young and Willmott were not merely content to quote figures for frequency of contact in their survey. They went into detailed descriptions of the form which such inter-household contacts took. The closeness of the relationships is well illustrated by the fact that in many instances two families shared so much of their daily life that they could be regarded, for some purposes, as a single domestic group. Married daughters were found to shop and eat regularly with their mothers and to depend upon them for all sorts of help and advice. The 'mums' played an active part in the rearing of their grandchildren. For the most part sons-in-law were also drawn into regular participation in the group, although they were also expected to keep in fairly close contact with their own families of origin as well. Townsend (1957), documents the way in which old people in Bethnal Green increasingly come to depend upon their children for help and support as age and infirmity weaken their independence, but emphasises the reciprocal aid which they themselves give whenever they are able. This is, of course, an extension of the relationship established after the marriage of a child. The special feature of the relationship for the aged, is their dependence or semi-dependence upon the children's families. This also illustrates the type of change which takes place in inter-household relationships, over time, but is quite clearly only one of many subtle and complex changes, the nature of which have not as yet been amply studied or documented.

Young and Willmott also investigated a sample of Bethnal Greeners, who had moved to 'Greenleigh', a new L.C.C. housing estate, some twenty miles away. They found that the traditional pattern of inter-household contacts had been disrupted by the move. Geographic separation has resulted in drastic decrease, both in the number and in the quality of contacts. Under the new pattern of visiting, married daughters were seeing their 'mums' about once a fortnight on average. Weekends were often set aside either for receiving or paying visits. The regular daily contact between members of the two families was replaced by mutual entertainment at much less frequent intervals, which served to reaffirm kinship links in the new situation, but nevertheless denoted a definite weakening of 'traditional' kin ties. Members of the husbands' families of origin were likely to be seen even less frequently, but the form of mutual visiting was essentially similar.

The differences between inter-household contacts in traditional working class communities and on new council estates are not altogether surprising. The barrier of distance tends to preclude daily contact between households of origin and households of marriage, on the new estates, though affectional ties may remain characteristically close, and in some cases even become stronger. The family moving to the estate is uprooted from its traditional setting, and re-established in a matrix of families, whose members are often at a similar stage of the life cycle. The majority of families moving to a new estate, during its initial stages, tends to be composed of married couples with young children, and the similarity of age structure tends to be maintained as they continue through the life cycle.

Newcomers to an established working class estate contribute to some extent to a diversification of age distribution, but even at Dagenham, forty years after its inception, the imprint of a skewed age distribution was unmistakable (Willmott, 1963). One of the most obvious practical problems arising from this was the creation of a disproportionate block of children of about the same age. This 'bulge' progressed first through infant, then junior, then secondary schools. The need for provision of extra jobs as the first wave of school leavers began to seek work, and the call for different types of leisure provision as both parents and children outgrew their respective 'youthful' pursuits, gave rise to further problems.

Willmott also found that children who had grown up on the Dagenham estate were no longer able to obtain a house on the estate easily. Local government legislation was in fact intervening to set a strict limit on the number of children who could establish their families of marriage on this estate of 90,000 inhabitants. After 1952, the L.C.C. restricted the annual quota of Dagenham houses available locally through Dagenham and Barking Borough Councils to 100, and a further 200 houses per annum were let to Londoners. Contrasting patterns of kinship linkage were found to exist between the former and the latter groups. The newcomers who had moved to the estate leaving their respective families of origin in the London area, were relatively isolated from their kin, and in many ways similar to those Bethnal Greeners who had moved to the 'Greenleigh' L.C.C. estate. The second group was composed of families of marriage in which the husband or wife, and in two thirds of the cases, both, had been reared in Dagenham. First degree relatives played an important part in the daily lives of this group, and Willmott was able to report 'In its essentials, this is clearly the same kinship system, transplanted from the bustling streets of the East End to the flat, open landscape of the Thames Estuary. Time has to a large extent restored the patterns of the past' (Willmott, 1963, p. 36).

The studies quoted so far have all been made in pre-dominantly working class areas. A similar study has been undertaken in Woodford, a middle class area, with a sub-stantial minority of working class families (Willmott and Young, 1960). There it was found that the patterns of inter-family contact were similar to those on the new 'Greenleigh' estate. Frequency of contact in Woodford was higher than at 'Greenleigh', but not as much as in Bethnal Green. It was found that middle class families used the motor car, the telephone, and letter writing as a means of contact, much more than their working class counter-parts. Middle class residences were also more likely to have a 'spare' bedroom to accommodate parents over-night.

Another study of thirty middle class households in the Highgate area of London provides more detailed informa-tion on contacts between married couples and their effect-ive kin. An attempt was made to relate each household's frequency of contact with certain genealogical categories of kin, to the geographic distance separating them. The outcome was that 'the only significant differences were found between members of the family of origin (and their spouses and descendants) on the one hand, and the rest of the kin on the other' (Hubert, 1965, p. 70). Some sort of contact was maintained with 81% of the kin in the former category, but only with 32% of the latter (for detailed tables see Hubert, 1965, pp. 71-72). The intensity and quality of contact was also found to vary between different categories of kin. Married couples tended to spend weekends or holidays with their parents at regular intervals. Contacts between siblings were generally not quite so intense but mutual weekend visiting did occur. Beyond this range of kin, however, contact tended to be different in kind, with very few cases of overnight stays.

Comparable data is also available for a rural community. In my own study of a Pennine Parish contacts between families of origin and a family of marriage were maintained over considerable distances. Offspring living as far away from Co. Durham as London or Portsmouth made a special effort to keep in touch with their parents, by writing regularly (about once a fortnight on average), and paying at least one visit to the dale during the course of the year. The majority of young migrants from the parish, however, did not move more than fifty or sixty miles away, and, on average, they returned to visit their families of origin once every 3-5 weeks. Visits in the other direction were much less frequent. Within the community itself, 65 out of a total of 167 households were involved in family of origin-family of marriage contacts. Such contacts were more frequent, more intense, and played an altogether more central part in the lives of both sets of family members, than contacts among with other kin. Mutual visiting was common. Mother-daughter contacts were not dissimilar from those in Bethnal Green, and the wife's contacts with her mother-in-law were also characteristically close, especially if her own mother was not alive, or lived elsewhere. Father-son relationships tended to be frequent and friendly, especially where a farm family was involved. The importance of the bond between father and son, has also been noted in farm families in other communities (cf. Arensberg and Kimball, 1948; Rees, 1950; and Williams, 1956).

This is the type of information which is currently available on inter-household contacts. Great emphasis is placed upon the relationship between the husband and wife, and their respective parents. Contact between a family of marriage and families of origin, however, may also involve grandparent-grandchild relationships, and intersibling relationships. Although the grandparent-grandchild relationship is usually regarded as a second degree relationship, 'one hesitates to say whether bonds which unite an individual with his grandchild are not sufficient to justify the inclusion of the latter within the first degree' (Rees, 1951, p. 74). This illustrates well the problem of trying to devise a satisfactory classification of kinship categories. Writings from several different sources indicate that the grandparent-grandchild relationship is usually characterised by strong positive affectional ties. Unfortunately the available evidence does not permit a more detailed analysis at the present time.

Contacts between siblings are usually most frequent and most complex while they share the same household. Insofar as contacts are maintained with the household of origin when a sibling leaves home, this is also likely to involve some inter-sibling contact. As successive siblings leave the household of origin, however, new axes of inter-household linkage have to be established, if contact is to be maintained. Contact tends to be somewhat reduced as successive siblings set up homes of their own and establish new interests and priorities. In Banbury, for example, 'there is some evidence to suggest that the parents are usually vital in keeping the married children together. When the parents die the family focus goes with them' (Stacey, 1960, p. 121). The Bethnal Green and Woodford material, and a recent study of Swansea (Rosser and Harris, 1965) also suggest that the household of origin tends to develop into an information passing centre. Siblings are at least kept informed about each other while parents, especially mothers, are still alive. At one further remove, the limited evidence available suggests that contact between the children of siblings (first cousins) tends to be considerably reduced after they leave their respective parental homes.

Only in contacts between families of origin and families of marriage is there any clear indication of the existence of widely acknowledged reciprocal duties, rights or obligations. Even these, when analysed in general terms, may be reduced to minimal obligations such as keeping in touch or giving help when required. Nevertheless it is a common research finding that in the majority of cases strong affective ties, and considerable reciprocal aid and support characterise family of origin and family of marriage contacts. The affective ties appear to be strong regardless of differences in social class background or geographical distance between households. Economic ties such as financial aid in crisis, participation in joint domestic groups for cooking and eating, and 'speaking for' relatives for housing or jobs have been reported between working class families of origin and families of marriage. The main economic considerations linking middle or upper class families of origin and families of marriage, however, may well revolve round property and inheritance, though it should be noted that middle and upper class parents often provide their children with substantial indirect economic assets such as 'an education', and 'social introductions'.

A tentative hypothesis which might be advanced at this juncture is that kinship links in the direct line of descent generate closer and more enduring social relationships between living kin than any other kin ties. The dependence of young children upon parents, and to some extent of aged parents upon adult children are obvious factors involved. Also inheritance and property considerations are undoubtedly highly correlated with direct descent (e.g. Crozier, 1965; Williams, 1963).

Kin ties other than those between households containing first degree kindred are not characterised by any generally recognised system of reciprocal duties and obligations. The principle of selectivity clearly comes into operation. Firstly, kin may decide whether or not to establish, or continue, a social relationship on the basis of a recognised kinship link. This type of decision is likely to be based upon shared economic, political, educational, religious or leisure interests rather than simply upon knowledge of kinship link. Secondly the form which a social relationship between kin takes can vary considerably, and is something which can be continuously worked out during the course of the social relationship.

The principle of selectivity, in relation both to the establishment and the content of social relationships between kin, is an extremely important feature of the British kinship system. But it makes the analysis of kinship ties extremely difficult, because of the great complexity and range of choice which is possible. This is well illustrated in the Highgate study where one of the major conclusions is that 'selection at each generation is highly significant for the apparently idiosyncratic nature of an individual's effective kin at any given point' (Hubert, 1965, p. 74). Further research into the complex factors which underlie the processes of selection is clearly needed.

So far relationships between kin have been discussed in terms of either inter-personal or inter-household contacts, because these are the predominant forms which such contacts take. Activities involving the participation of a larger grouping are comparatively infrequent, and are in most instances confined to sporadic meetings associated with birth, coming of age, marriage and death. On such occasion the 'corporate' group normally includes both friends and kinfolk, and where attendance is by invitation, selection from the network of effective kin is also possible.

Summary and discussion

One of the main problems in the study of British kinship structure is the lack of sufficient detailed information. Nevertheless certain concepts are clearly of considerable importance for kinship analysis. The concept of *the kin universe of a household* provides a general frame of reference. Within the kin universe certain categories of kin can be usefully distinguished. The *effective kin network* of members of each household can be reckoned either jointly or individually. For each individual, *kindred* can be distinguished from *affines*, kindred in the *direct* line of descent can be distinguished from those who are not, and *direct affines* can be distinguished from *indirect affines*.

An alternative but complementary way of looking at British kinship structure is as a series of interlocking nuclear families. This gives rise to the concept of differing degrees of kinship. Insofar as households are composed of nuclear family or partial nuclear family units the idea of degrees of kinship is particularly useful since the kin universe of a household can be viewed both as a series of interlocking nuclear families and as a series of interlocking households at the same time.

In Table 1 an attempt is made to set out the way in which degrees of kinship in an ego-centred network have been distinguished earlier in the chapter. It is perhaps worth noting that this is by no means the only possible set of definitions, but merely one that seems to be potentially useful to the understanding and analysis of British kinship behaviour. In the table first cousins of ego and ego's spouse, and merged affines are listed separately from distant kin because various authors attest their importance in British kinship structure. Strictly speaking, 'other kin' are not listed according to degree of kinship, but rather constitute residual categories.

Finally it should be emphasised that with the possible exception of intra-household relationships, the existence of a kin relationship does not necessarily lead to an ongoing social relationship. The principle of selectivity operates not only in the establishment and perpetuation of social relationship between kin, but also with respect to the form and content of such relationships, though from the evidence available it seems that social relationships with first degree kindred and affines, and members of their households, are established and maintained much more frequently than with any other categories of kin.

Table 1
Degrees of Kinship in an Ego-Centred Network

KINDRED	INDIRECT AFFINES	DIRECT AFFINES
(I) First Degree Kindred: ego's father, mother, siblings and children.		(I) First Degree Affines: ego's spouse, first degree kindred of ego's spouse.
(II) Second Degree Kindred: ego's father's parents and siblings, ego's mother's parents and siblings, ego's children's children ego's sibling's children.	(II) Second Degree Indirect Affines: spouses of ego's siblings, spouses of ego's spouse's siblings.	(II) Second Degree Direct Affines: second degree kindred of ego's spouse.
(III) Other Kindred: (a) first cousins (b) distant kindred (i.e. any other kindred).	Other Indirect Affines: (a) spouses of ego's parents' siblings, spouses of ego's spouse's parents, siblings. (i.e. merged affines.) (b) distant indirect affines. (Any other recognised indirect affines, including quasi-affines.)	(III) Other Direct Affines: (a) ego's spouse's first cousins: (b) distant direct affines. (Any other recognised direct affines.)

3

The developmental cycle: phases (i) and (ii)

Introduction

The nuclear family is the central structural unit of a conjugal family system. In the previous chapter some attention was given to the fact that nuclear family members tend to act as pivotal links in the establishment and perpetuation of inter-household contacts. It is now appropriate to focus attention upon the relationship between the nuclear family and the household as a domestic group. The household is certainly not the only form of domestic group to be found in Britain, but it is clearly the predominant one.

Certain facts concerning household size and composition are available from the Census of England and Wales. The census definition of a 'household' which is here equated with the domestic group, is 'one person living alone or a group of persons living together, partaking of meals prepared together and benefiting from a common housekeeping' (Registrar General, 1964a, p. X). There were 14,640,897 private households in England and Wales at the 1961 Census, containing 97% of the population. Approximately 6% of these households shared a dwelling with one or

more other households, but the proportions varied from
0·6% in rural areas to 14·1% in the conurbations. There
were only slight variations in household size between rural
and urban areas, and over 70% of all households contained
either two, three or four persons.

Much less information is available on household composition. In 1951, however, household composition in
terms of relationships to head of household was analysed
for a 1% sample of the population of Great Britain
(Registrar General, 1962). Estimates from this data indicate
that approximately 80% of households contain only
nuclear family members: this includes 13-14% of households in which persons live alone. Of the remaining 20%,
somewhat less than 5% of the households contain at least
two married couples, whereas the rest contain assorted
groups of persons, usually but not exclusively a core of
nuclear family members, plus additional persons.

Cycles of development

It is useful for purposes of exposition to distinguish three
forms of development cycle. The first is the developmental
cycle of the nuclear family. The second is the developmental cycle of the household. The third is the life cycle of
the individual. These are essentially three different perspectives from which to view the same sort of data.

The creation, development and subsequent disintegration of the nuclear family are well defined and familiar
processes. The major reference points of the cycle of
family development are, the public acknowledgement of
intent to marry, the actual wedding ceremony, the birth
(or adoption) of offspring, and the dissolution of the unit
which commences with the death of one member, and is

39

completed by the death of the last surviving family member. As previously noted each individual usually belongs to two nuclear families during his lifetime. His membership of his family of origin is ascribed at birth, and if he marries he acquires a second nuclear family membership in his family of marriage. Much confusion is caused by the fact that some authors use the term nuclear family in an ambiguous way. On the one hand, they refer to nuclear family members living in a single household as 'a nuclear family', on the other they refer to members of a nuclear family, wherever they live, as constituting a nuclear family. In this text the broader definition has been adopted, and the appropriate qualifications are made when the term is used in the narrower sense.

The concept of the developmental cycle of the household may help to clarify matters further. A new household is formed when an individual or group of individuals decides to establish an independent cooking and housekeeping unit, i.e. a separate domestic group. From that time onwards the household may either be augmented or be depleted by the gain or loss of members. The dissolution of a household group is achieved either by the dispersal of all members to other households, or by the death of a last surviving member. Nevertheless it is clear that the household may be perpetuated as a domestic group over several generations providing that some continuity of membership is maintained. The vast majority of households are comprised of kinfolk, and it is with this type of unit that we are primarily concerned. A third analytically distinct but closely related developmental cycle is the individual life cycle, which can be defined simply as an individual's life history from birth to death.

For any society one of the central problems in the

analysis of family and kinship, is to relate these three developmental cycles together. It is relatively simple to outline the manner in which the developmental cycles interlock, but comparatively difficult to achieve a satisfactory terminology, which does not conflict with much of the previous writing on the subject. The remainder of this chapter and the following chapter will be devoted to a discussion of the *developmental cycle of the household as a domestic group*, with special reference to households containing only nuclear family members. Rather than repeat this cumbersome phrase each time it is necessary to use it, a shorthand version '*the developmental cycle*' will be used throughout. It should be noted that this does not include the analytically distinct concept of the individual life cycle, which will be referred to as such in the following pages.

For purposes of description it is useful to think in terms of a normative developmental cycle, which can be used to analyse British data. Four major phases of the developmental cycle can be distinguished, (i) the courtship phase, (ii) the initial phase of marriage, (iii) the childbearing and childrearing phase, and (iv) the phase of disintegration. In the first of these, serious courtship brings together a man and woman from different nuclear families—their respective families of origin—and from different households which may or may not coincide with the families of origin. If marriage subsequently ensues, a new nuclear family is created. The wedding ceremony marks the end of the courtship phase, and the genesis of the family of marriage of the bride and groom. This initial phase of marriage is usually concerned with the consolidation of the new marital relationship and with the establishment of a home. Marriage does not, of course, always coincide with the setting up of a separate household, but it is normally expected that this will be a major preoccupation during the initial phase of marriage. The birth of the first child marks the beginning of the next phase of development. At this point the family of marriage of the new parents becomes, in addition, the family of origin of their offspring. The care of children during infancy, their socialisation and their material support until late adolescence, which occupy this third phase, are lengthy processes. The final phase approaches as offspring become involved in serious courtship, or plan to leave the domestic group for other reasons. The migration of offspring usually starts the phase of dissolution, and the death of either parent continues it. During the final phase 'the household as a domestic group' may in fact only contain one surviving spouse.

This highly generalised description of the normative developmental cycle provides the beginnings of a framework for the analysis of the British family system. Readers must bear in mind, however, that it is neither an accurate description of how all developmental cycles progress, nor is it in any way prescriptive, attempting to define how the developmental cycle should progress. It is merely an heuristic device intended to provide a simple framework for the analysis of the cyclical change of household composition insofar as such changes are related to kinship.

The normative sequence of the developmental cycle is not always followed in actual practice. There are many factors which lead to multiple variations in the pattern of development. The following variables are those which lead to deviations from the normative pattern in a substantial minority of cases: (i) failure to enter into serious courtship or to pursue courtship through to marriage, (ii) divorce, annulment, legal separation, desertion, and informal separation, (iii) early death of either spouse, or a child, (iv) infertility combined with a failure to adopt, and (v) the inclusion of persons other than the members of a single nuclear family in the domestic group.

The remainder of this chapter and the following chapter will be devoted to an assessment of the empirical evidence relating to the developmental cycle. It must be noted from the outset, however, that our knowledge on this subject is fragmentary and incomplete. Nevertheless it is useful to review the material currently available both for purposes of consolidating our present knowledge and for the guide that it provides for future research. Data has been drawn from official statistics; national, regional and local social surveys, and from a series of detailed community studies.

(i) *The courtship phase*

Contemporary courtship is marked by a high degree of informality. Arranged marriages and formal stylised courtship patterns are outmoded, and currently viewed with disfavour. The Victorian middle class idea of chaperonage has gradually given way to increased freedom of action amongst potential marital partners. Ideals of romantic love and individual freedom of mate selection have become an integral part of the ideology of courtship, if not of courting behaviour. The romantic love complex (Goode, 1959), which not only involves love as an expected element of courtship, but also contains the prescription that the foundations of marriage should rest upon mutual love, is probably a special phenomenon of 'Western culture', and is certainly one which has received *widespread* acceptance in Britain during the twentieth century. The combination of a relatively open choice system of mate selection and

43

comparatively informal courtship patterns, however, renders any analysis of courtship extremely difficult.

In the case of a single adolescent or adult, getting to know an eligible person of the opposite sex may be a prelude to a platonic friendship, or a preliminary to serious courtship. It is useful for analytical purposes to distinguish between preliminary courtship and the serious courtship which begins when a couple agree that marriage is decidedly in prospect. While courtship is in its preliminary stages, it is not unexpected that it should give rise to a number of ephemeral friendships. In fact such transient relationships have become an accepted part of modern adolescent behaviour. It is only with the onset of serious courtship that the developmental cycle begins in earnest, hence only this latter part of the courtship process will be given further consideration.

The major purpose of serious courtship is the exploration of the possibilities of marriage and future co-residence. The couple have an opportunity to assess their mutual compatibility, and throughout the period various interpersonal and external factors may either strengthen or weaken their resolve to marry. Generally speaking a couple gradually accumulate knowledge about each other throughout their relationship, hence the shorter the period of acquaintance and courtship prior to marriage, the greater the 'unknown' element to be revealed in marriage. Slater and Woodside (1951) found that 18% of their 100 'normal' married couples had known each other for less than one year, 61% for between one and four years, and the remaining 21% for longer periods. Those with a premarital acquaintance of less than a year proved to have significantly less happy marriages, according to their own perceptions of happiness. Chesser (1956) also concluded that in his sample of 1,026 married women, the chances of a happy marriage were *slightly* greater, the longer the period of premarital acquaintance.

Unfortunately there is very little reliable information available on how much time courting couples spend together, what they do during this time, and where they spend it. Premarital sexual behaviour is perhaps the one area which has received considerable attention in both serious and popular writing. It should be noted, however, that premarital sexual experience is obtained *outside* as well as within serious courtship, and that sex is only one of many considerations in courtship. Empirical studies, in Britain, tend to concentrate on actual sexual behaviour rather than upon standards, and much of the writing on premarital sexual standards derives from personal codes and official dogmas rather than from scientific investigation.

Illegitimacy is often taken as a reliable index of premarital sexual behaviour, but as far as serious courtship is concerned it can *at best* only indicate courtship failures. A small scale survey of 274 illegitimate births in a Midland city in 1949, provides some insights into the problems of interpreting illegitimacy statistics (Wimperis, 1960). In 57·5% of the cases investigated, there was a known bar to the marriage of the mother and father. Approximately 39% of the children were born of relatively stable consensual unions—i.e. unions in which the mother and father were living together as marital partners, though not legally married. From this evidence alone it is clear that this type of domestic group merits further research. The overall results of this survey suggest that illegitimacy is far more likely to be the result of extra-marital and pre-courtship behaviour, than the product of serious courtship. The results of this small survey though by no means

45

conclusive in themselves, are at least indicative of what the general situation is likely to be. Experienced social workers confirm that the figures quoted do not represent exceptional circumstances, though there are likely to be some differences on a regional or national scale.

A much more reliable index of the premarital sexual behaviour of couples engaged in serious courtship than the illegitimacy rate, is the proportion of premaritally conceived legitimate maternities. Such maternities accounted for 10·1% of all maternities in 1938, 7·7% in 1950, and 8·4% in 1962, in England and Wales. Recent figures show that 23% of all legitimate first births, and 40% of legitimate first births to mothers under 20 years of age, in England and Wales, were the result of premarital conception (Registrar General, 1965; see also Hartley, 1966). It is also interesting to note that premaritally conceived legitimate maternities, which in 1938 accounted for 70% of all extra-maritally conceived maternities, only accounted for just over 50% in 1963. These figures at least hint at a change in extra-marital sexual standards.

Reiss (1960) outlined four major standards of premarital sexual behaviour, (i) abstinence, (ii) double standard, (iii) permissiveness with affection, and (iv) permissiveness without affection. Though initially developed for the analysis of American standards these categories appear to be appropriate for the study of British standards also. Abstinence is a broad category involving as a minimum requirement abstinence from full sexual intercourse before marriage, but including various degrees of other sexually stimulating behaviour: (a) petting without affection, (b) petting with affection, (c) kissing without affection, (d) kissing with affection, and (e) complete absence of sexual contact. Petting in this context was defined as sexual behaviour more intimate than kissing alone, but falling short of full sexual intercourse. The major religious institutions in Britain clearly subscribe to a standard of abstinence, but are for the most part ambivalent in their attitudes towards the various degrees of abstinence. There is considerable evidence, however, that other sexual standards have a fairly wide currency in Britain.

The double standard, according to which a male is permitted intercourse prior to marriage, but a woman is supposed to remain a virgin, appears to have, or have had, the support of at least a substantial minority of the population. Implicit in the many reports of working class sexuality, is support for the double standard. It is interesting to note that the double standard, except insofar as it is self-contradictory, also implies highly permissive sexual standards on the part of at least a few 'mistresses' or prostitutes. The standard of permissiveness without affection, appears to have comparatively few positive adherents, except in this latter type of instance.

The emancipation of women and the associated emphasis on egalitarianism have both served to lower the appeal of the double standard. Circumstantial evidence suggests that permissiveness with affection is becoming a more acceptable public standard, especially amongst the younger sector of the population. In one sample of married women, the percentage who acknowledged that they had had premarital sexual intercourse rose from 19% of those born before 1904 to 43% of those born between 1924-1934, but it was noted that 'Many of the married women wrote in their replies that their premarital sexual experience was with their present husbands' (Chesser, 1956, p. 309; cf. Schofield, 1965, pp. 162-7). Nevertheless the various forms of abstinence still retain a major appeal as a formal standard. Gorer (1955), for example, in his survey of volunteers from amongst readers of *The People*, found that 52% of 4,983 respondents felt that a young man should definitely not have 'sexual experience' before marriage, and 63% of them indicated that a young woman should not have such experience. A recent survey of the sexual behaviour of unmarried teenagers aged 15-19 provides some basic information on premarital sexual behaviour in England and Wales. Sexual intercourse had been experienced by 20% of the boys, and 12% of the girls in the sample. The evidence indicates clearly that the older a teenager is the more likely he or she is to have experienced sexual intercourse (Schofield, 1965, p. 40).

It is clear that if romantic love is accepted as a major basis of serious courtship, only permissiveness with affection, and those parts of the abstinence standard which allow love are relevant standards for the intimate behaviour of a courting couple. Even if love were only accepted merely as an ingredient of courtship, the same would still hold. The dual standard, permissiveness without affection, petting without affection, and kissing without affection, separate sex from courtship. This serves to pinpoint the theoretical importance of love in relation to courtship and marriage, but gives no interpretation of why love should receive such special emphasis in Western culture.

The centrality of the romantic love theme in mate selection arises in part from the peculiarities of a monogamous multilineal conjugal family system. Love is often considered an important feature of a marital relationship in other systems, but nowhere is it idolised as the preferred basis of marriage, as much as in the conjugal system. Several factors contribute to this end. Firstly the absence of any generally recognised reciprocal duties and obligations between kin beyond the first degree means that most members of an individual's effective kin network have little vested interest in his or her marriage. Thus a premium tends to be placed upon the mutual compatability and adjustment of marital partners. Relatives, particularly parents, may still seek to influence an individual's choice of spouse, but in a conjugal family system tend to have fewer vested interests in doing so, compared with other types of kinship system. Secondly the field of eligibles is formally defined to include a wide range of adolescent and adult eligibles. Child marriage is proscribed by law. There is neither a closely defined system of preferential mating, nor of arranged marriage. Thirdly, the general norm of marital stability within a monogamous system, and a knowledge of individual responsibility for selection, is highly conducive to a pattern of courtship which stresses the importance of mutual trust and affection. The ideology of romantic love, therefore, tends to generate a high commitment to the socially approved form of marriage in a system in which wider kinship duties and obligations are not greatly emphasised.

Despite the absence of formal constraints on the field of eligibles, the prevailing tendency towards homogamy in the British kinship system has long been noted. Homogamy is marriage between persons of essentially similar backgrounds and interests. At the opposite end of this complex dimension it is possible to have heterogamy, or marriage between individuals with different social characteristics and interests. The social definition of the field of courtship eligibles tends to bias the selection of potential marriage partners. Couples rarely meet unless they have a minimum of social characteristics in common.

49

Similarities in social origin, achieved social status, place and type of work, educational experience, leisure interests and area of residence constitute the most important variables which tend to define the effective field of courtship partners. Moreover there is a high probability that similarities in one of these variables will either correlate with similarities in at least some others, or fail to constitute a sufficient basis for serious courtship.

Berent reported on similarities and differences in the social origin and educational background of married couples within a large stratified sample of the national adult population (in Glass, ed., 1954). A four point grading scale of occupations was used to compare marital partners in terms of their fathers' occupations. The spouses were also ranked on a four point scale of educational level. An agreement in either educational level or social origin was found in 83% of the marriages, including agreement on both items in 32%. Agreement in terms of educational level, however, was assured in 48% of the cases, given the distribution of husbands and wives over the four point scale.

From a theoretical point of view, it seems reasonable to hypothesise that similarities in major social background characteristics operate to define a substantial proportion of any one individual's potential marriage partners in an 'open' marriage system. The many British community studies lend support to such an hypothesis, but, because of their relatively limited frames of reference, provide no rigorous test of it. Both social and geographic mobility tend to widen the field of eligibles by increasing the range of contacts from whom a spouse is likely to be drawn. A recent American study, by Kerckhoff and Davis (1962), suggests that social background variables operate towards homogamy especially during the very early stages of the selection process, and that psychological factors are more important in the later stages. The same may well be true for Britain, but there is no adequate information available at the present time.

No introduction to contemporary courtship patterns would be complete, without a reference to engagements. Approximately 400,000 engagement rings are sold each year in Britain—a figure which is roughly equivalent to the number of marriages. A formal engagement has become the only 'respectable' prelude to marriage. The timing of an official engagement, however, is subject to considerable variation. For some couples the public announcement seems to coincide with their initial decision to marry, for others the period of 'informal engagement' may stretch from weeks to years, before a formal engagement is announced. Engagement practices appear to vary by social class, geographic area and individual preference, but there is little reliable statistical information on these matters.

(ii) *The initial phase of marriage*

In the present context of the British kinship system, 'marriage' may be taken to mean legal marriage. This both fulfils a minimum definition which requires that marriage is at least a union between two persons on the basis of which children are accorded a legitimate position in society, and at the same time specifies other conditions as well. Consensual unions do occur, but they form the basis of a relatively small proportion of household units. Relatively little systematic information is available on them and they will not be examined further. This is yet another field of investigation in which further research is required.

In Britain, the proportion of civil marriage ceremonies has increased from 2·6% of all marriages in 1844, to 29·6% in 1962. There has also been a redistribution of religious ceremonies over the various groupings and denominations. The proportion of Church of England ceremonies decreased from 90·7% in 1844, to 47·4% in 1962, whereas the proportion of Roman Catholic marriages increased from 1.7% in 1844, to 12·3% in 1962 (Registrar General, 1964b). The trend towards civil marriage is just one aspect of a wider tendency towards secularisation. There is no empirical evidence, however, which suggests that secularisation of the marriage ceremony *per se* has had any far reaching consequences upon marital behaviour. The hypothesis that civil marriage is positively correlated with high divorce rates, for example, still awaits verification.

A second major feature of contemporary marriage is the tendency for couples to marry at a relatively young age. The mean age at first marriage in 1962, was the lowest on record, 25·5 for bachelor grooms, and 23 for spinster brides. In 1961, 10·4% of all marriages were between minors. Such marriages accounted for 85% of bachelor grooms under the age of twenty-one, but only for 29% of spinster brides under that age. Calculations from divorce statistics show that marriages involving a minor are at least twice as likely to end in divorce, as marriages contracted between persons over the age of twenty-one. Several reasons have been suggested for this ranging from the immaturity of minors and their idealised conceptions of marriage, to an awareness that divorce is a viable alternative to remaining married. No systematic work has been carried out in Britain, but Goode (1956) in his excellent Wayne County study, suggests that there is no simple explanation for the pattern of American divorce. There is every reason to believe that the identification and systematic investigation of a complex set of causal variables is prerequisite for a systematic sociological analysis of divorce in Britain.

The trend towards marriage at lower ages has been facilitated by economic prosperity and comparatively high wages for young workers, but social rather than economic considerations are undoubtedly the main underlying factors. Marriage, for the young person in particular, may mark entry into adult status, and give rise to feelings of maturity, independence and responsibility. The ideology of romantic love, reinforced both by peer group contacts and the mass media, stresses that falling in love constitutes a basis for marriage. Adolescents, reared in a more permissive social environment than their forbears, expect to develop strong emotional attachments for contemporaries of the opposite sex, and many of them do. In times of economic hardship and deprivation, marriage may be *postponed* to later age, though the desire for marriage may be evident much earlier. Alternatively, certain sectors of the adolescent population, such as full-time students in institutions of higher education, may have a different order of priorities in which early marriage is relatively low on the scale.

Marriage usually involves a radical change in status for both bride and groom. The process of adjustment to the new status situation occupies a central place during the immediate post-marriage period. Husband and wife face the task of consolidating an intimate and demanding relationship. On an interpersonal level, the newly-weds develop their own pattern of eating, sleeping, sexual behaviour, and private leisure activities. The emerging routines of home life have to be integrated or at least reconciled with

53

participation in external work and leisure activities. The very fact of living together which, is an important corollary of most British marriages, produces stress and tension as well as mutual satisfaction and enjoyment. The delicate balance of marital harmony and discord is a product of the personalities of husband and wife, their expectations concerning marriage, their willingness and ability to adjust to each other, and their overall commitment to the marriage.

A prime concern during the initial phase of marriage would seem to be establishment or planning of an independent domestic group. Most newly-weds desire to begin their married life in a home of their own, and the majority appear to achieve this goal. One study reports that in a Liverpool sample of 275 households, covering all major status groups, 'as was expected almost all new families establish a separate new home immediately upon marriage. There were small differences in proportions in different groups, ranging between 80 per cent and 96 per cent, but these are not statistically significant' (Chapman, 1955, p. 40). On the other hand, there is considerable evidence to show that it was by no means exceptional for a working class couple to begin their married life in the home of either the wife's or the husband's parents, up to the end of the 1940s. A recent study of Swansea demonstrates that there may be considerable local variation. Of 625 couples married in Swansea between 1914-1960 and still living there in the early 1960s, 16% had shared a household with the husband's parents, and 34% with the wife's parents immediately after marriage. The proportion sharing a household with either set of parents showed an increase for those married between 1914 and 1939 (Rosser and Harris, 1965). These two studies provide evidence of local differences. The full range of information on the country as a whole can only be revealed by future research. A closely associated problem, which could be conveniently tackled at the same time, is that of the extent to which living in the same house leads to sharing the same domestic group.

Studies of rural communities and traditional urban working class areas, show that kinfolk are often instrumental in obtaining a home for the newly-weds. In Llanfihangel, for example, there is a general expectation that a farmer will help to provide for a son's home and livelihood. 'Unless the farmer had already acquired the tenancy of a second farm, he will assist his son to secure one, and he may pay the first six months rent' (Rees, 1951, pp. 64-5). In Bethnal Green, the bride's mother was found to play an important role in 'speaking for' a home for her daughter: 'She asks neighbours, she asks other relatives of hers, she asks her own rent collector and others in the street, she asks the publican and shopkeepers, she asks the estate agents' (Young and Willmott, 1957, pp. 23-4).

The pattern is quite different on the 'new estates', however, where for the most part the intervention of kin loses significance, because of the way in which local councils draft their rules and 'point systems', for the allocation of tenancies. The Dagenham estate, during its early phases, was atypical in this respect. Even on privately built new estates it seems that kin linkages at an inter-household level may be comparatively few in number. In 'Winston Parva', for example, the lack of local kinship ties on the twenty year old private estate contrasted markedly with the strongly developed network of kin ties in the 'old village' zone of this suburban area (Elias and Scotson, 1965). The estate, however, was inhabited by working class tenants. In contrast, relatively little is known about the part played by kinfolk in helping young couples to embark upon owner occupation. The upper or middle class parent, in particular, usually has more resources at his disposal to offer advice and financial assistance on owner occupancy, but the degree to which such resources are utilised is unknown.

Establishing a home is part of the much wider process of developing a life style. The decisions which the newly married couple have to make about the use of their resources in building up their material possessions tend to be simpler than those involving their new pattern of social relationships. The matrix of kinfolk, friends and acquaintances of the newly-weds is usually modified during the initial phase of marriage. Pre-existing social relationships are given a new perspective by the marriage bond. Very often bride and groom find themselves faced with conflicting sets of expectations from various groups and individuals within their social networks. Such dilemmas may bring the newly married couple into conflict with each other, and/or lead to a change in the composition of their effective social networks.

The development of clearer expectations between husband and wife as to how the other will behave in a given situation is a gradual process, which may be described as marital socialisation. It should not be assumed, however, that the process of marital socialisation necessarily gives rise to marital harmony. A husband or wife may strongly disapprove of a spouse's behaviour, yet come to expect it, and even to defend it from attack by others. This is often the case, for example, when a husband takes to regular 'excessive' drinking, an unrealised first stage of alcoholism. Marital socialisation obviously occurs throughout the length of a marriage relationship, but it is hypothesised that it is of particular importance during the initial phase. Such evidence as there is suggests that the type of relationship established immediately after marriage strongly influences the subsequent pattern of relationships throughout the remainder of the marriage, although there is clearly a modification of the type of activities involved as the couple progress through the developmental cycle.

Many attempts have been made to analyse different patterns of conjugal relationships. A contrast is sometimes attempted in terms of two major stereotypes of 'family structure' in Britain. In the first of these, the 'patriarchal family', the husband is usually portrayed as an authoritarian head of household, and the relationship between husband and wife as that of superior and subordinate. The 'Victorian family' as described in early London surveys, approximates to this description (Mayhew, 1851; Booth, 1902). The other stereotype, that of the 'companionship family', presents an ideal of joint decision making and egalitarianism as far as husband and wife are concerned. It is often assumed that there has been a gradual change from patriarchal to companionate structures. The middle class are regarded as the leaders in this change, the traditional working class as the diehards clinging to a patriarchal style of organisation. These are sweeping generalisations which are not supported by available empirical evidence.

The work of Bott provides an excellent framework for an examination of this problem. She suggests a distinction between (i) segregated conjugal role relationships, and (ii) joint conjugal role relationships. In the former case activities are carried out by the husband and wife, either without reference to each other, which in Bott's terms constitutes 'independent organisation', or as part of a distinctive division of labour, which constitutes 'complementary organisation'. With joint conjugal relationships, the same activities are pursued by husband and wife together, or by either spouse at different times (see Bott, 1957).

The following description of segregated conjugal relationships is taken from an account of the 'mining family' in a traditional working class community.

> With the exception of a small minority of men who spend a good deal of time pottering about with household improvements or are passionately interested in some hobby, or are newly married, the husbands of Ashton for preference come home for a meal after finishing work and as soon as they can feel clean and rested they look for the company of their mates, i.e. their friends of the same sex (Dennis, Henriques and Slaughter, 1957, pp. 180-1).

On the subject of leisure activities and the performance of household tasks the same authors conclude: 'The point about all these and other activities is that in no case do they demand co-operation or encourage the growth of companionship between husband and wife' (ibid., p. 183). The husbands and wives of 'Ashton' clearly organise their activities on a complementary rather than an independent basis, and this probably represents an extreme of complementary organisation in Britain.

In several other long established working class communities there appears to be a trend away from segregated conjugal relationships, if the historical material is accurate. The trend is clearly outlined for Bethnal Green, 'There is now a nearer approach to equality between the sexes and, though each has a peculiar role, its boundaries are no longer so rigidly defined nor is it performed without consultation' (Young and Willmott, 1957, p. 15). Working class couples in Woodford were found to be similar to their counterparts in Bethnal Green. In contrast, however, it was found that the majority of middle class husbands in Woodford '. . . as well as doing much of the heavy work in the home, carrying the coals and emptying the rubbish, act as assistants to their wives for at least part of their day' (Willmott and Young, 1960, p. 21).

Community structure, geographic mobility, type of effective kin network and class background appear to be related to the organisation of marital relationships, but the exact nature of the inter-relationships between all these variables is unknown. Bott's analysis of the conjugal relationships of twenty married couples living in the London area gave rise to an important central hypothesis, that 'the degree of segregation of conjugal roles is related to the degree of connectedness in the total network of the family. Those families that had a high degree of segregation in the role-relationship of husband and wife had a close-knit network; many of their friends, neighbours, and relatives knew one another. Families that had a relatively joint role-relationship between husband and wife had a loose-knit network; few of their relatives, neighbours and friends knew one another' (Bott, 1957, p. 59). Bott's work requires further clarification, but at least provides a reasonable starting point for analysis.

At the present time it is possible to draw certain tentative conclusions about the relationship between community structure and style of marital relationship. It should be noted, however, that the structure of kinship networks and of wider social networks is an important component of community structure. New estates are characterised by a high rate of in-migration during the early period of their establishment, and incoming households usually become geographically separated from other households in their respective kin networks. Under these circumstances, there appears to be a relatively uniform trend in the patterning of husband-wife relationships, regardless of class background. On the Barton Estate, for example, there was much less segregated activity than in the long-established working class neighbourhood of St. Ebbes, from which many of the estate families were drawn (Mogey, 1956). On a Liverpool estate it was found that there was more shared activity between spouses than there had been in the old established areas from which the population had been drawn (Mitchell, Lupton, Hodges and Smith, 1954). There is also evidence of joint conjugal relationships at Dagenham, which with a population of over 90,000, has been described as the largest working class estate in Britain (Willmott, 1963).

As far as rural communities are concerned, it seems that a segregated but complementary conjugal relationship is likely to be found on small family farms (see Rees, 1950; Williams, 1956; Turner, 1967). Evidence on rural non-farm households is inconclusive. Data on long established urban communities suggest that, for the most part, middle class couples are more likely to exhibit joint conjugal relationships than working class couples. The work centred executive of Woodford, and the home centred miner of 'Ashton', however, should indicate that this tendency is by no means uniform. Moreover it is possible that factors such as rates of migration and the existence or absence of strongly developed local networks of effective kin may account for the apparent differences between working class and middle class urban communities. The existence of such complicating variables is well illustrated by contrasting the Bethnal Greener who is 'surrounded not only by his own relatives and their acquaintances, but also by his own acquaintances and their relatives' (Young and Willmott, 1957, p. 82) with the Highgate couples. In Highgate it was found that 'it is not only our informants that have moved from their parental home or home area, but the majority of their kin have scattered too, in this and the previous generations' (Hubert, 1965, p. 65).

4
The developmental cycle: phases (iii) and (iv)

The courtship and initial phases of marriage tend to occupy a relatively short period of time, when compared with later phases. The childbearing and childrearing phase alone often accounts for the greater part of the time occupied by a particular family and household in the developmental cycle. The final phase of dissolution also tends to occupy a greater time span than either of the two early phases, particularly with the increasing expectancy of life, and the tendency towards a relatively young average age of marriage.

(iii) *The childbearing and childrearing phase*
Approximately 10-14% of married couples in Britain never give birth to a child. Childlessness is attributable to a variety of causes. There are those who cannot reproduce, either for physical or emotional reasons, those whose marriages are terminated by death, divorce or separation before conception occurs, and those who deliberately choose not to become parents. Childless couples are represented in the divorcing population 2-3 times more frequently than in the married population generally, though

absence of children is not necessarily the factor leading to divorce. In many instances the same incompatibilities which lead to the divorce court, may also be the main factors underlying the absence of offspring. Despite the relatively high proportion of childless couples sueing for divorce, however, it is significant that the proportion seeking to adopt children is substantially higher. In 1964, for example, there were 10,509 divorces in England and Wales, compared with about 14,000 legal adoptions, among childless couples (Registrar General, 1966). Nevertheless this still leaves a very substantial proportion of spouses who remain together without children.

The developmental cycle of this latter group of childless couples differs radically from that of people who take on parental responsibilities. The upbringing of children usually places substantial demands upon both the material resources of the household and the time and energy of the parents. The socialisation of children is in itself a lengthy process and parents may be involved in it for between 15-40 years, depending upon the number of children, the time elapsing between successive births, and the period of dependency of each child. Generally speaking, therefore, childrearing occupies a considerable proportion of what may be regarded as the parents' most active years of adult life. Childless couples are free, during this same period of their lives, to channel their time, energy, and resources into alternative lines of action. A 'compensatory principle' has been noted in several instances, according to which a childless couple sometimes take a great interest in children of kinfolk or close friends, and as indulgent 'uncle' and 'aunt' occupy a position analagous to that of grandparent. Other couples appear to expend their energies in different directions, into their occupations, their hobbies, their homes, voluntary work, and other leisure activities. It remains for future research to reveal the processes by which such choices are made.

The overwhelming majority of married couples, however, do have children. For them, the arrival of the first child, in particular, marks not only the beginning of a new generation, but also a radical change in social commitments. The fact that the mother and father reorient themselves and are socialised into their parental positions is often neglected, the major emphasis being placed upon the socialisation of children. The incorporation of the position of mother alongside that of wife clearly amounts to a substantial modification in the structure of household relationships. The restrictions of pregnancy, and subsequent recurrent needs of the new infant during the first few months after birth, serve to curtail the mother's activities outside the home. The working wife normally gives up her job, and finds her freedom to engage in leisure activities severely circumscribed. The new mother-child relationship is intensified by the obvious dependency of the infant, and the period just before and after birth is one of considerable emotional involvement for the mother. The birth of the first child thus generates a new family position for the mother, and one which has considerable repercussions, not only on her other kinship positions, but also on her multiple societal positions as well.

The development of the relationship between father and child tends to be somewhat detached from the immediate circumstances of gestation, birth and early physical dependency. It seems from the available evidence on patterns of child rearing, that typically the British father develops his new relationship with the infant rather slowly, and compared with the mother is only in direct contact with the baby for relatively short periods each day. Indeed the father in a household where strict conjugal role segregation prevails may claim that the care of the child is none of his business, and may ignore the infant whenever possible. On the other hand, the more closely the husband-wife relationship approximates to extreme joint conjugal role organisation, the greater the likelihood that the husband will devote more time to developing his relationship with his offspring. The Newsons, in their survey of 709 Nottingham families, specifically enquired about the father's role in the care of one year olds. They report differences in the father's rate of participation in child care according to occupational background. Participation was highest among white collar and professional and managerial fathers, somewhat lower amongst skilled and semi-skilled manual workers, and clearly lowest amongst unskilled workers (Newson and Newson, 1963, p. 213).

The arrival of a second or subsequent child usually does not have the same type of impact as that of the first. The parents have their previous experience upon which to draw, and their style of life has already been adapted to the presence of a child in the social environment. In fact, of the three family members, father, mother and first child, the latter appears to face by far the greatest problems of adaptation and adjustment. Nevertheless, each successive child places extra demands upon parental time and household resources, and thus gives rise to a general reorientation of family relationships. While the arrival of a new baby marks a definite point of change, it is necessary to stress that parents are *continuously* reorienting themselves as the children undergo the process of socialisation. The way in which parents react to both new

65

demands and changing circumstances of the child's development is a most important factor, both from the parents' and the child's point of view.

From an emphasis upon the effects of the arrival of the child upon the parents, it is now appropriate to turn to a much more conventional and widely documented topic—the effect of family background upon the socialisation of the child. Both psychologists and sociologists have long been interested in this topic, but it is still an area in which partial theories abound, and no single one is generally accepted as pre-eminent. This is perhaps due in part at least to the difficulty of integrating sociological and psychological theories.

Alongside those elements of British society which are common to most of the population, there is also considerable diversity in material possessions, styles of life, and modes of thought and language. Where the local situation is such that a social group with relatively homogeneous values can be identified, a sub-culture may be said to exist. In considering the socialisation of children, it is necessary to bear in mind that a child is born not only into a particular household situation but also into a particular neighbourhood, and often into a distinguishable sub-culture as well. The great diversity of sub-cultural contexts that exist in England, is well brought out in *Samples from English Cultures* (Klein, 1965). In the second volume of her study, Klein attempts to explore systematic differences in child-rearing patterns. The main conclusion that one is left to draw from Klein's work is that childrearing practices vary according to differences in the sub-culture, or local area, and that it is useful to classify sub-cultures in terms of their social class composition.

The newborn child knows nothing of the society into

which he is born. He is extremely dependent upon others for the fulfilment of his basic needs for survival. His behaviour patterns are only developed to a rudimentary extent, and within the general limitations of intelligence and physical capability, the child can be moulded to fit vastly differing sets of social positions in a wide range of societal and sub-cultural contexts. The process of communication is extremely varied but it is clear that parents, especially the mother, are usually the most influential individuals during a child's early development. The early formative experiences are encountered mainly in the context of home and family, or at least in social situations in which the mediation of household members is required. The norms and values of a sub-culture and of the wider society, therefore, are selectively communicated to the child through household members. Household members do not only act as filters and transmitters of norms and values, however, they also establish idiosyncratic standards as well, but it is only when a child communicates with non-household members that this might become apparent.

There is some evidence to suggest that a child does not develop a relatively coherent frame of reference before he reaches the age of eight or nine, even for organizing his attitudes and values concerning so familiar and limited a sphere of action as that of household behaviour. The child's value system therefore is one which contains numerous discrete sets of norms, attitudes and values, which do not necessarily show internal consistency. It is only as the child matures mentally that values tend to become grouped into a relatively small number of wider value constellations, and even in the adult, internal consistency of values is extremely rare.

Parents usually seek a high degree of conformity from

their children. In part conformity is spontaneous and constitutes no problem, but in part strategies and techniques of social control have to be applied in order to ensure conformity. Strategies of control are based upon a manipulation of a child's mental and physical environment. A child, of course, develops counter strategies, usually of a more limited kind—e.g. playing off one parent against another. Allied with parental strategies are two major techniques of social control. Firstly there is physical coercion, that is either threat of physical punishment or the actual use of physical force. Secondly there are 'psychological' techniques such as the withdrawal of love. This, of course, presupposes a strong emotional attachment between parent and child. Both of these methods enjoy considerable use in Britain today, sometimes separately but usually in combination.

As far as the parental techniques of control are concerned, it seems that the premium on physical coercion is greater among traditional working class families, than amongst middle class families, amongst whom there is a greater reliance on 'psychological' techniques of obtaining conformity. Recent work (e.g. Spinley, 1953; Newson, E., 1963) supports this general view, but also makes it quite clear that the distinction is by no means simple and clear cut. Techniques of social control do vary with social class, but they also vary according to the age and personality structure of the parents, and according to the area in which the parents live. These latter factors cut across class distinctions to some extent. Changes through time complicate the picture further, because the use of psychological techniques appears to be on the increase amongst both working and middle class parents.

Parents are the key figures throughout the early socialisation of the child up to and perhaps including puberty and adolescence. Despite a parental monopoly of authority over the infant, however, socialisation is a haphazard process. Only in comparatively few respects do parents consciously set out to train their children in any systematic way. For the most part the infant learns from his experience of living in a particular home environment, which is oriented towards providing, to some extent, for the wants and needs of all family members, not just for those of the infant. As the child grows older, individuals outside the nuclear family and experiences outside the home become increasingly important in the socialisation process. Parents, however, have the authority to exert considerable influence on these other agencies of socialisation, the most important of which are the peer group, the school and the mass media.

Family, peer group, education institutions and mass media function in highly complex interrelationships in the socialisation process. In the early stages of child development, at least, parents exert an overriding control over the child's exposure to socialising influences. Parents can choose whether to let children under five play with peers, whether to send them to a kindergarten or pre-school play group, and whether to allow or encourage them to pay attention to the mass media, particularly television. The middle class trend in Britain appears to be in the direction of active parental encouragement of social participation outside the home and selective use of mass media. In sharp contrast 'respectable' middle class parents, at the turn of the century, closely controlled and restricted their children's contact with peers, but readily subjected them to the supervision of domestic servants. In working class homes, survey data indicates that for at least two or three generations parents have encouraged their children to spend leisure time with their peers, and elder siblings, particularly sisters, have been expected to look after younger brothers and sisters.

Compulsory education beginning near the age of five exposes the child both to the influence of the teacher and of his peers in a social context which is fairly remote from the home and family. The norms and values of a child's network of peers, of his teachers, and of his parents almost inevitably differ at some points. The part played by the mass media is somewhat ambiguous as norms and values of the family, school and peer group, are not only selectively emphasised in the media, but also selectively perceived by the child. Thus in the areas of conflict, mass media may reinforce the norms and values fostered by parents, peer group, or teachers, or may in each case reinforce certain norms and values but not others. Nevertheless it is quite clear that during the period of primary education the various influences which impinge upon the child serve to widen his social horizons well beyond the limits of family life, and thus provide the foundations for subsequent independence from family of origin, and possibly from community of birth also (e.g. Parsons, 1951, pp. 240-2).

In Britain it is generally expected that parental control will remain firm at least until a child reaches adolescence. Adolescence may be conveniently viewed as a transitional phase in the individual's life cycle in which he is moving out of childhood relations and beginning to assume some of the hallmarks of adult status. When children reach adolescence, this also sets the foundations of a transitional phase for the family as a domestic group. The adolescent tends to become less dependent upon his parents either for emotional or material support. A phenomenon labelled 'adolescent rebellion' frequently occurs. This involves the rejection of parental authority, and more generally the rejection of any adult who continues to treat the adolescent as being of less than full adult status (i.e. according to the adolescent's own perceptions of the way he is being treated). Adolescence and adolescent rebellion are extremely complex topics which merit treatment in their own right (see Grinder, 1963).

In Britain, where it is usual for newly-weds to attempt to establish their own domestic group upon or soon after marriage, the presence of adolescents in the domestic group marks a relatively mature stage in the developmental cycle. Parents are usually still active adults and their children are progressing rapidly towards adult status. This state of affairs usually heralds the onset of fission in the domestic group. Members of the younger generation enter the courtship phase, and the phase of disintegration of their family of origin as a domestic group rapidly approaches.

(iv) The phase of disintegration

For the present purpose of dealing with British data, the phase of disintegration will be taken to refer to the period over which the nuclear family core of a household unit breaks up. In the majority of instances, the phase of disintegration commences with the departure of a household member to a separate domestic group, as for example when a son or daughter leaves the parental home, or when a spouse secedes from the domestic group. In other cases the death of a family member marks the beginning of the disintegration phase.

When a son or daughter leaves the parental home it is

usually to start upon specialist training, a new job, or marriage. Activities within the household may have to be reorganised, but it is probably true to say that most British parents who find it difficult to reorient themselves to the 'loss' of children from the domestic group, are reacting primarily in terms of sentiment. The death of a household member, however, especially if it is one of the parents, often gives rise to problems of succession and inheritance. Who takes over the role of breadwinner or housekeeper, as the case may be? How are activities reorganised to cope with the loss? As far as property is concerned, there is little published sociological research on this topic (but for one example see Williams 1963, pp. 79-83). Nevertheless this is clearly an important area for future sociological research. Questions which require clarification are—what forms of property are held? Which member(s) of the household have legal title to them? Who inherits when one spouse dies? Who inherits when both are dead? The whole problem of death, succession and inheritance is perhaps a difficult one to investigate, but a considerable volume of knowledge on these matters has been accumulated for other societies.

There are certain 'social formulae' which, theoretically at least, help to deal with the 'crisis' of a son or daughter leaving home. In the case of marriage, the engagement, the wedding preparation, and the ceremony and ritual of the wedding day constitute a socially accepted way of preparing the parents for their 'loss', as well as providing for a public acknowledgement of the change in status of the bride and groom. A second formula, though much less formal, is simply for parents to regard a child's absence from home as temporary. This often appears to be effective in helping parents to adjust to the situation in which a child leaves home without marrying. Almost any researcher enquiring into household composition is familiar with cases in which unmarried offspring living away from home are listed by their mothers as belonging to the household. The offspring themselves may, of course, either incline to the same viewpoint as their parents, or may consider their departure from the parental home as no less final than if they had in fact married.

It is generally regarded as a usual pattern of events for an adolescent or adult to leave the parental home. If a husband or wife decides to leave, however, this is commonly viewed as a breakdown of the domestic group. Statistics are available for dissolutions of marriage and for legal separations. These indicate that for every 1,000 married couples in Britain, 2 or 3 divorces, annulments or legal separations occur each year. Over 50% of such breakdowns occur within the first eleven years of marriage. In these instances, the phase of disintegration of the family as a domestic group commences more quickly than is usually expected, and may run concurrently with the early childrearing phase. However, it is important to realise that the majority of divorcees remarry. This means that the developmental cycle, though disrupted by divorce, is subsequently recommenced with a new courtship and marriage. Unfortunately there are no reliable statistics available on the number of broken marriages which occur without resort to legal action. It seems highly probable, however, that this type of broken marriage is at least as frequent as legally sanctioned broken marriages.

The death of a household member may also occur at a relatively early period in the developmental cycle. When this occurs the phase of disintegration may also be regarded as running parallel with earlier phases. The death of a child may, in fact, have little effect upon the developmental cycle, providing that there are other offspring living or subsequently born. This obviously does not mean that family members do not suffer a sense of personal loss in such cases. The death of an only child, which is followed neither by a subsequent birth nor by adoption, obviously leads to a serious disruption of the normative developmental cycle.

Widowhood during the early childbearing and childrearing phase constitutes yet another deviation from the normative cycle of development. The results of a Bethnal Green survey of 72 widows bereaved in youth or middle age, highlights some of a widow's problems of adjusting to her bereavement and attempting to establish a new pattern of life (Marris, 1958). Marris describes the process extremely perceptively.

At first the loss of her husband seems to spread a pervasive mood of frustration over all a widow's interests. For a while she may become indifferent even to the care of her children: her home, her future, her family—nothing matters any more. Bewildered by her loss, she can hardly at first believe it. She still hears his footsteps on the stairs, his voice calling, finds herself waiting for him at the door when men come home from work, and as each habitual expectation is unfulfilled, she begins to realise the meaning of his death. Then she may cling all the more desperately to her memories, to his possessions, trying to deny that he is really gone, only to feel grief all the more poignantly when the power of illusion fails. Or she may try to escape from everything that reminds her of the past. But this seems a betrayal of the dead, and in its turn arouses all her latent anxieties about the sincerity of her love, the fear that she is in some way responsible for his death, even

74

absurdly wished it. And she may defend herself against these self-accusations by an obsessive assertion of her grief. Thus bereavement seems to involve a conflict between a desire to acquire an indifference which the loss has no power to hurt, and to idealise the happiness of which it deprived her (Marris, 1958, pp. 124-5).

Although Marris' sample consisted of widows bereaved in youth or middle age, it is unlikely that the sentiments of widows who have shared a longer period of married life will be less complex. In fact a reasonable hypothesis would be that the older a widow at the time of bereavement, the more serious are her problems of adjustment. Unfortunately much less is known about the effects of widowhood upon widowers. Economic problems facing the widower are likely to be comparatively less severe, whereas the problems of child rearing and socialisation are likely to be more complex. Remarriage provides a means for both widows and widowers to start a new family cycle in the context of the old domestic group. It appears, however, that the majority of widows and widowers, even of those under the age of sixty, do not remarry.

The position of old people during the phase of disintegration appears to vary considerably, from one domestic group to another. Unfortunately many researchers into ageing in industrial societies, often choose to study the process from the time people reach pensionable age, i.e. when the domestic group is most likely to be somewhere near the middle of the phase of disintegration of the developmental cycle. In fact an awareness of the structure of a domestic group immediately prior to the onset of disintegration, and an analysis of the total process of disintegration are vital to a clear understanding of the ageing process. In some cases the continuity of the domestic group is preserved, in others it is not.

When the continuity of the domestic group is not preserved, this is due to a combination of children leaving the parental home and the death or migration of their ageing parents. In such cases the domestic group may be nominally represented by one widowed parent until it is finally dissolved, and the family property is transmitted to the heirs. It appears to be fairly common for ageing parents, especially widowed parents to relinquish their homes and join the domestic group of one of their offspring or even of other kinfolk, when they feel that they can no longer fend for themselves. The widowed parent thus joins a domestic group which already has its own authority structure. Generally a son or son-in-law is head of the household and a daughter or daughter-in-law, mistress of the home. The aged parent, therefore, often assumes a fairly marginal role in the domestic group, when joining during old age.

Sometimes aged parents manage to preserve continuity of membership in the household as a domestic group. This is the case for example, when a child marries and brings a spouse to live in his or her parents' domestic group. The continuity of the domestic group is maintained because as one nuclear family unit is dissolving, another is simultaneously expanding to take its place. In the past this three generation type of structure appears to have been fairly common during certain phases of the developmental cycle. Nowadays, however, it seems to be comparatively rare, except as a 'temporary' expedient, when married offspring are unable or unwilling to establish an independent domestic group. The continuity of the domestic group is sometimes preserved by an unmarried child remaining with aged parents, or a widowed parent, and subsequently inheriting the home. In this instance, however, the continuity of the domestic group is fairly slender, and even if the child marries when both parents are dead, the overlap between his or her family of origin and family of marriage is reduced to a minimum. It is interesting to note that when the continuity of the domestic group is preserved, parents of the senior generation usually remain 'master and mistress' of the household until their death, that is, they nominally at least continue to hold superior authority positions in their own domestic group.

There is growing evidence to show that the majority of ageing couples with children are not isolated from them. The Swansea study contains a useful analysis of the final phase of the cycle of family development (Rosser and Harris, 1965, ch. viii). The statistics, which refer only to persons of pensionable age, show that approximately half of the parents with living children share accommodation with them. Widows and widowers lived almost twice as frequently with their married offspring as aged married couples. The differences between proportions of widowed parents and married couples living with unmarried offspring, however, are not statistically significant. Data from several other studies, summarised in 'Postscript 1963' to *The Family Life of Old People*, show that between 52 and 69% of aged parents live in the same dwelling as at least one of their children, and that less than a quarter of the old people surveyed did not have one or more children living nearby (Townsend, 1963, p. 238, Table 28). Old people in institutions comprise less than 4% of those of pensionable age. Nevertheless there appears to be a fairly high turnover in such establishments, and the plight of these old people constitutes an increasing social problem (see Townsend, 1962).

One final aspect of family disintegration, about which little is known, merits consideration. There are domestic groups which comprise 'empty shell families' (Goode, in Merton and Nisbet, 1964, ch. 9). Goode defines an empty shell family, as one in which some or all of the family members fail to fulfil their duties and obligations to one another and reduce their social contacts to a minimum. Insofar as family members just continue to live in the same dwelling, but fail to operate as a single domestic unit, such empty shell families do not constitute viable domestic groups. The number of empty shell families in Britain is unknown, and particularly difficult to discover, because of the intimate knowledge concerning close inter-personal relationships which is required. It is reasonable to hypothesise that many empty shell families will be dissolved by (i) annulment, divorce, or legal separation, and (ii) desertion, or mutually agreed informal separation of husband and wife. The proportion of dissolutions in this latter category is also unknown. Similarly the pro-portion of legal dissolutions preceded by an empty shell structure of family relationships remains undisclosed. Ignorance of the number of families which perpetuate an empty shell structure, without dissolution of the marriage, must also be admitted. Finally the phase at which an empty shell structure develops is uncertain. This is an important topic, into which research is urgently required.

Summary and discussion

An attempt is made in Table 2 to summarise the conceptual framework of the developmental cycle. The idea of a

Table 2

The Development Cycle of the Household as a Domestic Group with special reference to nuclear families as household units.

'NORMATIVE' PATTERN	FORMS OF 'DEVIATION'
(i) *Courtship Phase* Begins with serious Courtship. Ends with Marriage.	A. Continued failure to enter serious courtship. B. Termination of serious courtship prior to marriage. C. Contraction of a 'consensual union'/'de facto' marriage.
(ii) *Initial Phase of Marriage* Begins with Marriage. Includes establishment of a separate domestic group. Ends with birth/adoption of a child.	D. Failure to bear/adopt a child. E. Divorce : Annulment. [Re-marriage possible.] F. Legal separation. G. Enduring informal separa-tion/desertion.
(iii) *Childbearing and Child-rearing Phase* Begins with birth/adoption of a child. Shades into next phase. Ends when offspring achieve 'adult' status.	H. Emergence of an 'empty shell' family structure. I. Death or serious illness of one or more family members in phase (ii) or (iii). [Remarriage may follow death of a spouse.]
(iv) *Phase of Disintegration* Begins with dispersion of offspring, or death of parents. Continues with dispersion or death of family members. Ends with dissolution of nuclear family as a domestic group. [In certain cases continuity of the domestic group is preserved, i.e. two or more developmental cycles over-lap with same household as focal centre.]	J. Acceptance of unrelated persons into domestic group on a contractual basis. (e.g. lodgers : evacuees.) K. Acceptance of kinfolk and/ or friends into domestic group. (See p. 80 for a com-ment on this category.)

normative development cycle provides the point of departure, and common forms of 'deviation' from the normative pattern are indicated. Once again it is perhaps worth emphasising that both 'normative' and 'deviation' are here used in a statistical and not in a prescriptive sense.

Two questions which immediately spring to mind are: (i) How many households containing nuclear family units follow the normative developmental cycle? (ii) How important is each of the modes of deviation? If forms of deviation J, and K (i.e. the addition to the domestic group of persons outside the nuclear family core) are omitted from the calculation, it is possible to arrive at the following quantitative estimates. Approximately 65-70% of the adult population appear to follow the main sequence of the normative developmental cycle. It must be admitted, however, that while these domestic groups may be composed only of the members of a particular nuclear family unit during most of the developmental cycle, it is not unreasonable to hazard a guess that many of them will be expanded by the addition of non-nuclear family members at some time in the cycle. Indeed future research may well demonstrate that such expansion of the domestic group over fairly short periods is, in fact, normative.

The experience of the remaining 30-35% of the adult population in respect of the developmental cycle can be broken down into the following five categories:

  (i) 8-10% of males and females who never marry. (Forms of deviation A, B, and C.)
 (ii) 9-10% of married couples who fail to rear children but do not obtain a divorce, annulment or legal separation.
      (Form of deviation D—this estimate excludes a further 2½% of married couples without children

who obtain a dissolution of marriage or a legal separation.)

(iii) 7-8% of married couples who obtain a divorce, annulment, or legal separation.

(Forms of deviation E, and F.)

(iv) 5-10% of married couples who do not obtain a divorce, annulment, or legal separation, but who develop an 'empty shell' family structure and/or become permanently or 'semi-permanently' separated.

(Forms of deviation G, and H.)

(v) Less than 1% of couples for whom death or serious illness disrupts the developmental cycle in the initial phase of marriage or the early part of the childbearing and childrearing phase.

(Form of deviation I.)

These estimates are relatively crude and therefore subject to possible error, but at least they provide a guide.

Certain trends are worth noting. Firstly the proportion of the age group 45-49 remaining unmarried has fluctuated between 8·5% and 12·5% during the present century. Recent marriage statistics, however, indicate that a higher proportion of people than ever before are either getting married, which means that there will be fewer bachelors and spinsters in the 45-49 age group in the future. Secondly, dissolutions of marriage, as expressed in the annual divorce rates have increased from 0·2% to 7% since 1900. There is no evidence to suggest that divorce rates will show a decline in the immediate future. It is difficult to extrapolate a trend in respect of childless couples. Such variables as earlier age of marriage, proportion of children available for adoption, medical advances in the treatment of sub-fertility, dissemination of the idea and means of birth control, and remarriage would need to be carefully analysed. A further problem arises with empty shell family structures and permanent extra-legal separations. My estimate of 5-10% is based on very slender evidence. The trend is certainly unknown. It is possible to argue either that the rise in the divorce rate is counterbalanced by a decline in *de facto* broken marriages, or alternatively that the rise in the divorce rate is a genuine reflection of a trend towards an increasing proportion of both *de jure* and *de facto* broken marriages.

Finally a general comment concerning the notion of 'sequence' in the developmental cycle is perhaps warranted. Contemporary ideas of a cycle of development imply both the progression of events through time, and the repetition of similar sets of progressions (i.e. cyclical repetition). It should be evident from the foregoing discussion that *there is no rigid chronological sequence of events in each particular developmental cycle, but that multiple variations are possible within a fairly general overall sequence.* One of the major difficulties in attempting an analysis of the developmental cycle in relation to empirical data, stems from the fact that no longitudinal studies covering the developmental cycle of a sample of domestic groups from beginning to end have yet been carried out. This text like most others dealing with the household as a domestic group relies on information collected over relatively short periods of time. Obviously at any one point in time there are domestic groups in all the different phases of development in Britain, but it is possible that there may in fact be important differences from generation to generation. Little is known about the process of modification which takes place with the repetition of successive cycles of development. The scope for future research in this field is enormous.

5

Kinship and social structure

Introduction

The sociologist who devotes his attention to the study of kinship has to delimit his field of investigation in some way. The 'real world' from which the sociologist draws his 'data' is extremely complex, and the models of kinship structure which he attempts to build are extremely simple by comparison. The approach adopted in the present text comprises an attempt to identify kinship positions, and to examine relationships and sets of relationships between them, as well as salient activities associated with them. It is important to note, however, that most of the activities mentioned are not exclusive to kinship positions, and that it has been necessary to refer to many non-kinship positions in order just to outline selected aspects of kinship structure. It is therefore appropriate to turn to a brief consideration of some of the ways in which kinship structure is related to the wider structure of British society.

One way of conceptualising social structure is as an extremely complex network of social positions. No complete catalogue or classification of social positions exists, in part because of the enormity of the task, and in part because of the multiplicity of possible approaches. Sociologists, however, often attempt a rough classification into educational, economic, kinship, political, recreational, and religious positions. This is by no means an exhaustive classification, but it is broad enough to cover most of the social positions and sets of social positions, to which sociologists have usually devoted their attention. In the present chapter, a brief examination of the relationship between kinship structure and the wider structure of British society will be attempted from two viewpoints. Attention will be focused upon the effects of increasing specialisation of activities and differentiation of positions upon kinship structure. At the same time some illustrations of the inter-relationships between educational, economic, political, recreational and religious activities and kinship structure will be attempted, though it should be noted that relatively few systematic studies of these relationships have been made.

There is a discernible trend towards increasing specialisation of activities in many spheres of social life, and a concomitant tendency towards increasing differentiation of social positions. The complex processes underlying these trends are not really understood at the present time, but the trends themselves are evident not only in Britain, but in many other nations also, and illustrations are relatively easy to find. In Britain, for example, the growth of large scale factory production and of intricate systems of distribution and exchange of goods and services on both a national and international level has been accompanied by increasing specialisation of economic activity and proliferation of different occupational positions. Similarly the development of complex large scale organisations in other fields such as politics, education, religion and recreation has contributed towards increased specialisation and differentiation.

Goode, in a recent study, has suggested that patterns of change are discernible in kinship systems 'in the direction of some type of *conjugal* family pattern—that is, towards fewer kinship ties with distant relatives and a greater emphasis on the "nuclear" family unit of couple and children' (Goode, 1963, p. 1). He clearly points out that the trend is more noticeable in some societies than others, and that there are considerable fluctuations and variations within the overall trend. The limited evidence available on changes in British kinship structure over the past hundred years indicates that alterations have taken place in the general direction suggested by Goode. This overall trend can be discussed conveniently in the light of the more general trend towards specialisation of activities and differentiation of social positions.

Differentiation of social positions and kinship structure

A kinship system provides one basis upon which an individual may build up his social network. In small scale societies with comparatively simple material cultures, kinship can easily supply the dominant organising principle for social life. Allocation of social positions can be made on the basis of an individual's position in the kinship system. But the likelihood of a reasonable 'fit' between the patterning of kinship, and economic, political, religious, or leisure activities decreases with the development of a more complex society. The major spheres of social life tend to become more insulated from each other, and specialisation of activities leads to proliferation and differentiation of social positions, and hence to an increasingly complex structure of social relationships within a society. When highly complex and differentiated social structures have developed, kinship is only likely to provide the basic structural principle underpinning social relationships for members of certain special groups such as the British Royal Family, or a large 'family firm'.

The social significance of kinship depends upon the extent to which it provides a basis for social relationships. In Britain, the kinship system is structured and operated in such a way that all of an individual's recognised kin rarely, if ever, come together as an exclusive group. Rites of passage—christenings, initiation, marriage and funeral ceremonies—are sometimes referred to as events which bring together an individual's kin as a corporate group, but it should be noted that in the majority of instances the guests on such occasions constitute a group of selected or self-selected kinfolk and unrelated friends. Nevertheless, rites of passage do provide a basis for reaffirming the existence of kin ties, and to a lesser extent they help to introduce the young persons present to genealogical complexities.

Generally speaking, however, relationships within the wider kin group tend to be diffuse and selective. Some differentiation of kinship positions from economic, educational, political, recreational and religious positions has clearly occurred, and the net result appears to be that there are very few, if any, rights, duties and obligations which are generally associated with relationships between distant kin. In fact, unless common political, economic, educational, religious or leisure interests cement ties of kinship between second degree or peripheral kin, the product of common social descent or affinity is likely to be mere social recognition, rather than a close social relationship. Insofar as the more distant bonds of kinship are becoming less important, in industry, politics, education, religion and leisure activities, such ties are increasingly unlikely to give rise to effective social relationships. It must be noted, however, that, although it appears possible to infer an overall trend towards the decreasing importance of second degree or more distant kinship links, it is hardly possible to make a serious attempt at *measuring* the trend because of the inadequacies of the data.

There are some difficulties in assessing the significance of kinship linkages in the fields of political, economic, educational recreational and religious activities. An analysis of the kinship connections between certain 'top decision makers' in the fields of banking, insurance, politics, and public administration provides a good example of the sort of problems involved (Lupton and Wilson, 1959). The initial focus of the study was upon persons involved in the Parker Tribunal (i.e. Bank Rate Tribunal, 1957), but the research was extended to cover six categories of 'top decision makers'. At least 18% of these 'top decision makers' proved to be related by blood or affinity. The actual ties linking any 'top decision maker' to any other, undoubtedly constituted only a small proportion of the ties in his kinship universe, and his kin ties probably coincided with only a small proportion of his total links with other decision makers. This immediately raises the problem of how to assess the significance of the kin ties that were demonstrated. Were kinship linkages an important factor, either in helping an individual to become a 'top decision maker', or in the actual decision making process? A provisional answer can be suggested to the first part of this question, but at the present it would be mere speculation to attempt an answer to the second part.

Many studies demonstrate that family background and kinship connections are two sets of variables influencing an individual's position in economic, educational, political and leisure institutions. But they also firmly indicate that family and kinship variables are merely a few amongst many, which need to be considered. In the *British Political Elite*, for example, it is suggested that family influence and connections are more likely to be important in helping Cabinet Ministers to their first steps on the political ladder, than during subsequent phases of their careers (Guttsman, 1963, p. 217). It is also evident that 'influential kinship connections' are not a prerequisite for holding Cabinet office in contemporary Britain.

The implications, which may be restated in a more general form are that in non-kinship institutions, kinship ties may or may not be of importance. When they do assume a special significance it is quite likely to be because kinship provided the basis of initial personal contact, and the ensuing social relationship developed within a kinship frame of reference. There is little evidence to suggest that the existence of kinship ties provides a basis for determining the content of non-kinship activities. The possibility remains, however, that in a particular social situation an individual will act in the interests of his kin, in what can be socially defined as a non-kinship context.

The distinction between kinship activity *per se*, and non-kinship activity which involves kinsmen, presents considerable analytical problems. It is theoretically possible to distinguish between (i) the rights and obligations which are generally accepted as part of particular kinship roles, (ii) mutual expectations which develop from an initial basis of kin roles—these can be termed quasi-kinship expectations, and (iii) rights, obligations and expectations which accidentally or incidentally involve kin. In practice, it is more difficult to apply these categories. Rights and obligations involved in specific kin relationships may be defined differently according to such variables as social class, proximity of residence, age, personality, etc. This is a matter for empirical investigation. It is somewhat more difficult to analyse the way in which kinship and non-kinship activities and interests interlock in complex social situations. Even in cases where kinship linkages are superimposed upon existing relationships, as for example. when the 'up and coming young executive' marries his managing director's daughter, there are considerable problems involved in attempting to assess the significance of kin ties. Nevertheless it is arguable that if kinship ties are specifically recognised they are potentially of significance in any social context.

The general impact of increasing specialisation of activity and differentiation of social positions, therefore, appears to have led to a decline in the significance of linkages between second degree or peripheral kin. The degree of selectivity permitted in the establishment and perpetuation of social relationships with these categories of recognised kin is of interest in this context. On the one hand, it suggests that kinship ties constitute somewhat less of a basic organising principle in economic, political, educational and recreational activity than they did, for example, in Victorian times. On the other hand, there is fairly strong evidence to indicate that shared economic, political and recreational interests coincide with the existence of social relationships between recognised kin, which suggests that the sentiments of kinship are not in themselves sufficient basis for the continuance of social relationships between kin. There is so little systematic evidence available, however, that it remains for future research to explore and modify these ideas.

The nuclear family and the wider social structure

Under the impact of the same influences which have affected the wider kinship system, the social positions of nuclear family members appear to have become increasingly specialised. Relationships within the household as a domestic group and between nuclear family members generally, have become more precise and less diffuse in content, as also have relationships between other kinfolk. The difference, however, is that the minimum expected level of activity within the domestic group, and to a lesser extent between nuclear family members not sharing the same household, continues to provide an adequate basis for the perpetuation of social relationships, which are usually construed in a kinship framework, whereas the minimum expected level of activity between more distant kin often fails to provide any such basis. It is perhaps worthwhile, therefore, to attempt to outline some of the ways in which the specialisation of economic, political, religious, educational and recreational activities is associated with specialisation of activities within the household and the nuclear family.

The effects of economic development and occupational diversification have recently been summarised as productive 'of a system of stratification becoming increasingly fine in its gradations and at the same time somewhat less extreme and less rigid' (Goldthorpe and Lockwood, 1963, p. 134). A particularly noteworthy feature has been the great increase in the proportion of white collar positions over the past hundred years—i.e. clerical, administrative, intermediate managerial, and minor professional occupations. At the same time the material standard of living has tended to rise for all groups in the population, and some writers claim that there has been a reduction of extreme economic inequalities. The rate of intergenerational mobility between strata has also increased.

An individual derives his initial class position from his family of origin. The occupation of the head of household is perhaps the most widely used index of social class for all members of the nuclear family. It has been well established that the residential area, consumption patterns, type of authority structure, income, educational background and the general style of life of a nuclear family, are significantly correlated with social class position, as defined by occupation. Goldthorpe and Lockwood, however, have put forward the hypothesis that middle class and working class styles of family life are undergoing a process of independent convergence.

> Spelled out in more detail, this argument would claim that convergence in attitudes and behaviour between certain working and middle class groups is the result, primarily, of changes in economic institutions and in the conditions of urban life, which have weakened simultaneously the 'collectivism' of the former and the 'individualism' of the latter (Goldthorpe and Lockwood, 1963, p. 152).

At the household level certain changes have occurred which are clearly associated with occupational diversification and the increasing complexity of the economic structure. The contemporary household tends to be more of a unit of economic consumption and less of a unit of economic production than formerly, though there are a few notable exceptions such as the households of small farmers, independent tradesmen and shopkeepers. The separation of home and place of work which is one element contributing to the above trend, also has several other consequences. The location of the home is usually strongly influenced by the place of work of the main breadwinner in the household. Geographic mobility is often encouraged by opportunities for occupational mobility and by the concentration of industry in certain locations.

Family life within the household unit becomes focused upon domestic activities such as cooking, housekeeping, gardening, child socialisation and a host of leisure interests. Division of labour and economic specialisation have also resulted in an increasing variety of available goods and services. This has tended to discourage homegrowing of basic foodstuffs and home production of goods from raw materials. At the same time, both the quantity and variety of domestic appliances in 'mass production' have multiplied, and such appliances have come within the purchasing power of the majority of households.

Changes in the economic structure during the past 150 years have been paralleled by changes in political structure. The extensions of the franchise and the emergence of politics as a full time occupation both inside and outside Parliament, together with the changing structure of local government, have been accompanied by widespread changes in the form and content of political participation. Political socialisation is neither a necessary aspect of household activity, nor a monopoly of the nuclear family, but it is evident that family background can be an important factor in political socialisation. This is particularly likely to be the case when a nuclear family or kin network contains active political figures. On a more general level it appears that a child is likely to derive at least an initial predisposition to support particular political ideologies from his parents, and that adult members of a household may well influence each other's participation in political activities.

The widening of the franchise and the 'professionalisation' of politics have also been accompanied by a general expansion of state control in many areas of social life. The state now endeavours to exert control in areas which were previously acknowledged to be within the sphere of influence of 'the family', the wider kin group, and the local community. In England and Wales legislation bearing directly on nuclear family relationships is becoming increasingly common. One form of welfare legislation is well illustrated by the various Children Acts, and Children and Young Persons Acts. These have imposed limits on the freedom of parents, to treat their children as they wish. The minimum duties of the parents, which conversely constitute the rights of the children, are clearly defined, and penalties specified for infringement of the law. Property rights of family members, and the right of a spouse to economic support constitute further examples within this category. The distinctive feature of this type of legislation is that obligations and sanctions are clearly specified and rigorous enforcement of the law is attempted.

A second form of welfare legislation is concerned with the guarantee of a certain 'minimum' level of subsistence, and the provision of special benefits to meet contingencies such as unemployment, sickness, and old age. National Insurance, National Assistance and Old Age Pensions, clearly come within this category. A third aspect of welfare legislation which impinges upon the individual and the nuclear family is concerned with the provision of what the State defines as 'socially desirable facilities'. The National Health Service and the State Education System, are two outstanding examples of this type of legislation. It is worthy of note that no individual or family is forced to use these facilities. Private education, private medical facilities and private means of support in time of unemployment, sickness, and old age are not prohibited.

The state also controls the establishment of legal marriage, and sets out in considerable detail the conditions under which, and terms upon which, a marriage can be dissolved. The State defined marriage, as a public contract undertaken in the Anglican Church or exceptionally in a Jewish or Quaker setting, by the Harwicke Act of 1753. It was not until 1836, however, that civil marriage, or marriage in other non-conformist establishments was legally recognised. The ecclesiastical hegemony over dissolution of marriage was first broken by Private Act of Parliament in 1697. But it was not until the Matrimonial Causes Act of 1857 that there was a general civil, as opposed to religious, recognition of dissolutions.

Marriage and divorce legislation provides one example of the State taking over temporal powers from the Established Church. This is just one relatively minor feature of a widespread trend towards secularisation. The general expansion of state control at the expense of religious bodies has rendered overt religious participation much more voluntaristic than formerly, and has also facilitated the rise of new sects and denominations. The history of organised religion in England and Wales over the past two hundred years is extremely complicated and there have been important regional differences. The effects of these intricate changes upon family life, and the part played by the family in the process of secularisation, however, remain relatively obscure.

Insofar as it is possible to generalise, it is necessary to make a distinction between rites of passage and rites of intensification. The former give religious recognition to birth, coming of age, marriage and death, focal points in both the developmental cycle of the household as a domestic group, and the individual life cycle. The latter are concerned with the regular reaffirmation of a wider range of religious beliefs, and take the form of religious services and public or private acts of worship. With the exception of religious 'coming of age' ceremonies, which have tended to become increasingly divorced from secular 'coming of age', rites of passage continue to play an important role in family life. Despite the ready availability of civil marriage, the proportion of persons rejecting, or excluded from, a religious ceremony has increased but slowly. Baptisms, christenings, and funerals remain an even more important religious preserve.

The rites of passage of a religious association, especially of a church or denomination, can and often do operate as a means of ascribing a child to that particular association. Almost invariably the parents are responsible for the initial choice of a child's religious affiliation. Even if a religious group consciously rejects the idea of committing a child to membership by infant baptism, the parents are usually responsible for the child's general orientation to religion. Hence it is not surprising to find that most religious groups stress the importance of 'the family' in religious life. There are some common themes such as the sanctity of marriage, but for the most part different religious ideologies give rise to varying expectations concerning family behaviour. The Exclusive Brethren and the Jews for example, insist that marriage should not take place with members of other faiths. Roman Catholic doctrine stresses that the child of a mixed Catholic and non-Catholic marriage should be brought up in the Roman Catholic faith. The Church of England officially subscribes to the view that divorced persons should not be allowed to remarry in Church. These are merely commonplace examples. It is possible, however, to analyse in detail the moral teachings and ethical codes of religious associations in relation to family behaviour, and to attempt to measure the degree to which these variables are interrelated. Unfortunately, this task remains largely unattempted for Britain, and is clearly outside the scope of this text.

Despite the ascriptive aspects of religious affiliation and the fact that an overwhelming majority of the population participate in rites of passage at appropriate times, regular participation in rites of intensification is confined to a distinct minority. Attempts have been made to gauge attendance at rites of intensification by a 'Sunday census' system, by counting Easter communicants, and by assessing average attendance figures over a set period. Estimates based on the slender evidence available suggest that less than 25% of the adult population attend public rites of intensification once a year or more. The exact percentage, if known, would probably be less than this. It also appears that attendance at rites of intensification has definitely declined during the past hundred years, although there have certainly been fluctuations in the trend, both within and between sects and denominations, and in different geographic areas. Rites of intensification in the home are even more of an unknown quantity. How prevalent are family devotions? How far do broadcast services bring religion into the home? These are just two of the myriad questions upon which a sociologist requires more information before he can begin to assess the general relationship between religion and family life. It is surprising how few facts are available in this field.

It is interesting to note that in all State aided schools children are required to attend a daily corporate act of worship, unless their parents choose to have them excluded. In this instance state legislation, while obviously favouring some forms of religious instruction, accepts that the parent with deep religious or anti-religious convictions should be able to make the final decision about his offspring's participation in an act of worship. This choice is but one of many to which the parent has a right under the 1944 Education Act. There is an obligation upon the parent to see that each child receives a 'full time education suitable to his age, aptitude and ability'. But the parent may choose to send a child to a state school or an independent school, or alternatively to provide some form of home tuition (see Burgess, 1964).

It is significant that most parents tend to accept the education offered by the State through the Local Education Authorities, often without any conscious attempt to use their prerogatives, and leave decisions about their children to professional educational administrators and teachers. There is a definite class bias in this respect. Not only do upper and middle class parents make comparatively less use of the State system of education, but they are more fully aware of the range of possibilities open to them even within the State system. Middle or upper class parents are also likely to be more articulate in pursuit of what they consider to be 'good educational facilities' for the children, than working class parents.

Family background can also be an important variable

in educational achievement. Children from working class backgrounds tend to be at a disadvantage relative to their middle class counterparts even in the State system (see Bernstein, 1958 & 1959; Douglas, 1964; Floud *et al.*, 1957; Frazer, 1959). The most commonly recognised forms of disadvantage for the working class child, when ability is held constant, may be listed as follows:

   (i) limited home vocabulary—spoken English often far from grammatically correct (especially important when early streaming occurs);

  (ii) less accustomed to control by psychological techniques at home, but exposed to this type of control at school;

 (iii) less stress is given to the importance of educational achievement at home (even where there is emphasis on achievement, working class parents are, generally speaking, less able to give their children constructive aid);

  (iv) intelligence tests often show a small but definite bias in favour of the middle class child;

   (v) norms of 'middle class teacher' are likely to require greater adjustment from the working class child;

  (vi) peer group of working class child from a distinctly working class area is likely to reinforce expectations of relatively poor academic performance (continued academic success can lead to social ostracism);

 (vii) economic advantages of leaving school at fifteen years of age tend to appear relatively more attractive for the working class child.

In some cases these factors tend to operate cumulatively, whereas in others they do not. Some can undoubtedly be attributed to differential education of parents, others

98

depend upon the extent to which there are significant variations between middle class and working class norms and values. The impact of the disadvantages can also have a differential effect according to the ability of the child. In some cases it may mean the difference between two streams in the same school, in others it may mean a difference between a grammar school education and an alternative form of secondary education, and yet in other cases it may make little substantive difference. Finally, a word of caution, these factors by no means operate in every case, and though they are more commonly found amongst children from working class backgrounds, they are by no means exclusively limited to that stratum.

There is no doubt, however, that the differential impact of family background upon educational opportunity and achievement is much less marked than it was before the 1944 Education Act. This is an important point to bear in mind because educational qualifications are coming to play an increasing part in the admission of individuals to particular kinds of job and to vocational training schemes. The introduction of the Certificate of Secondary Education opens up the possibility of a future demand for formal qualifications of entry for semi-skilled and possibly even for unskilled jobs. This means that educational achievement is likely to emerge as an even more important avenue of both upward and downward mobility, than it is at present. The role of the nuclear family and the domestic group in the educational process, therefore, is likely to be a crucial topic for future sociological research.

Changes in economic, political, religious and educational institutions have also been paralleled by changes in leisure patterns. Most writers on the topic seem to agree that both time and resources available for leisure pursuits have shown a considerable increase from the early 1950's to the present day. Rural community studies indicate that mutual informal visiting was, and possibly still is, a major leisure activity for many families. Such visiting patterns appear to be successively less important in traditional working class communities, middle class suburbs, and new estates, though the evidence for this is rather impressionistic, supported as it is by few studies of what may possibly be non-representative areas.

The major change in leisure patterns has undoubtedly occurred in the field of 'organised leisure'. In one sense the intrusion of the mass media into the home illustrates the spread of organised leisure, albeit in a loosely structured way. Outside the home the network of organisations and businesses catering for leisure activities is continually expanding. It is worth noting that the individual seems to be regarded as the basic consumer unit, although there are 'family entertainments' and 'family facilities'. Expansion of recreational facilities has also led to increasing specialisation—to clubs and voluntary associations with extremely specific and limited goals—which tends to exclude family participation.

Leisure patterns are also clearly associated with type of family and social class background. Participation in formal voluntary associations is primarily associated with middle class background, but it must be noted that by no means all middle class adults participate, and working class adults are not excluded. In contrast working class leisure activities tend to be much more loosely structured and informal. Two factors, the income differential and the status differential, clearly underpin this distinction. The overall trend towards the expansion of organised leisure, however, seems to be having a similar effect upon both working class and middle class families, though the processes involved seem to be different. There has been a decline in the proportion of leisure time devoted to shared family activity relative to that devoted to individualistic participation in organised leisure activities.

The extent to which household members spend their leisure time together is not well documented, nor is any clear distinction usually drawn between leisure and routine domestic activities, which makes it extremely difficult to generalise further. But it seems logical to assume that there will be some general variations in patterns of shared leisure activity according to the phase of the developmental cycle through which a household is passing at a given point in time, but it is likely to be some time yet before very much systematic information is available on the relationship between household, nuclear family and leisure.

Summary and discussion

It is evident, even from the present brief outline, that the relationship between kinship institutions and other institutions in the social structure is extremely complex. Most of the topics mentioned in this chapter could easily merit a substantial text in their own right, and the literature pertaining to them is vast, though in many writings, family and kinship factors are usually treated as incidental to the main theme. No systematic, theoretically grounded, empirical study of the part played by family and kinship variables in British social structure is currently available. Indeed, such a study would constitute a major advance beyond the frontiers of contemporary sociological knowledge.

6
Conclusion

This introduction to the study of the family and kinship system of modern Britain has been in part an introduction to sociological concepts, and in part a review of the available literature. The main aim, however, has been to present a rudimentary conceptual framework for the analysis of kinship structure and behaviour. Data has been drawn primarily from sources on England and Wales, but has occasionally been supplemented by references to Scotland and Ireland. Given the present state of knowledge, it is too early to attempt systematic regional comparisons, although there are clear indications that this would prove a useful and interesting future undertaking.

Five major approaches to the sociological and social-psychological study of marriage and family life are distinguished in *Handbook of Marriage and the Family*. These are (i) the institutional approach, (ii) the structural-functional approach, (iii) the interactional approach, (iv) the situational approach, and (v) the developmental approach (see Christensen, ed., 1964). Some elements of all these approaches are to be found in this book, but insofar as any one predominates it is an eclectic developmental

102

approach, although the institutional and structural-functional underpinnings are manifest. The interactional and situational approaches are not really represented more than would be generally expected with a developmental approach. These orientations stem in part from the adoption of a sociological rather than a psychological approach, and in part from a desire to devote more attention to kinship structure and behaviour outside the nuclear family than is customary in a text dealing with a modern industrial society.

Elements of the developmental approach, which are commonly found in American sociology, are apparent in the use of concepts such as the cycle of family development, the individual life cycle, and the processes of socialisation of children and adults. Analysis in developmental terms, however, is considerably strengthened by the incorporation of the structuralist concept of the developmental cycle of the domestic group, which is a distinctive contribution of British social anthropology. The heart of the conceptual framework adopted in this text is contained in the notion of the developmental cycle of the household as a domestic group, with special reference to households containing only nuclear family members (see Table 2, p. 79).

The influence of the structural-functionalist approach is perhaps best illustrated by the inclusion of a section on the wider kinship structure, and by the brief mention given to the interplay of kinship and other aspects of social structure. Nevertheless it should be emphasised that the 'functionalist' implications have been largely ignored, and attention has been primarily focused upon the 'structuralist' contribution. The relatively formal analysis of kinship positions as ego-centred networks of kindred and affines, and as sets of interlocking household and nuclear family units, constitutes an attempt to provide some of the foundations for a developmental approach to kinship networks (see Table 1, p. 37, and Appendix, pp. 108-112). A detailed analysis of the way in which kin universes and effective kin networks of households change through time is necessary to this type of developmental analysis. Unfortunately data of this nature is not yet available, and material relevant to this topic was introduced under the headings of *Social contacts between kin* (pp. 25-35), and *The initial phase of marriage* (pp. 51-61), rather than within a systematic developmental framework. Similarly, the chapter on *Kinship and Social Structure* was presented mainly by way of illustration, although the empirical generalisations about increasing specialisation of activities and differentiation of social positions clearly fit in with a developmental and structural approach.

The so-called institutional approach, insofar as it is relevant to contemporary sociological studies of family and kinship, might be re-labelled 'historical and comparative method'. The present text is based explicitly upon the assumption that the study of kinship structure and behaviour in contemporary Britain can most profitably be viewed in the broader perspective of kinship studies in different societies during various historical periods. This in itself is merely one aspect of the sociologist's more general concern with the comparative analysis of social structures and behaviour in differing time and space perspectives.

Analysis at the comparative structure level is extremely complicated, and fraught with major theoretical and methodological difficulties. Ideally analysis of this type requires that two significant problems are solved simultaneously. Firstly there is the problem of identifying the key dimensions of kinship structure, which would yield information about variations in the kinship structure of different societies, and of achieving satisfactory measures of these dimensions. General areas in which some, at least, of these dimensions are to be found—social descent, affinity, and the structure of domestic groups—were briefly outlined in the introductory chapter. The second problem concerns the extent to which any correlations can be established between particular measures of the dimensions of kinship structure, and particular measures of the dimensions of other aspects of social structure. By implication this second problem involves the satisfactory comparative analysis of social structures generally, and thus anticipates considerable development in the theory and methods of contemporary sociology.

For heuristic purposes, it is convenient to distinguish four levels of analysis in the field of kinship studies:

(i) The comparative analysis of social structures and behaviour.

(ii) The analysis of the relationship between a particular kinship system and the social structure of which it is part.

(iii) The analysis of the internal structure of a particular kinship system.

(iv) The analysis of the developmental cycle of domestic groups of kinfolk, within a particular kinship system.

Each of these successive levels of analysis is more limited in scope than the previous one, and is subsumed under the prior heading. The first two levels are clearly beyond the scope of the present text, but are important for the sociologist or potential sociologist who wishes to concentrate upon kinship analysis. As is perhaps appropriate for an introductory text, emphasis has been placed upon the next two levels of analysis; i.e. upon the analysis of the British kinship system as a system in its own right, and upon the developmental cycle of the household as a domestic group with reference to nuclear family units.

In conclusion certain key points about the British kinship system can be summarised. Kinship affiliation is based upon the principles of selective multilineal reckoning of descent, and of serial monogamy. These principles operate in such a way as to give rise to a conjugal family system. The nuclear family is a unit of central importance in this system. Most individuals belong to two nuclear family units in their lifetimes. They are born into their families of origin, and acquire membership in a second nuclear family upon marriage. It is convenient to conceptualise British kinship structure not only in terms of relationships between an individual and each member of his kin network, but also as a series of interlocking nuclear families, in which direct intergenerational links, the main axes of property inheritance, are of special importance. It is also necessary to take into account the fact that a high degree of selectivity is permitted in the establishment and perpetuation of active social relationships between recognised kin. In fact only when nuclear family members are involved as pivotal links between kin does there appear to be any widespread expectation of regular association between kin.

Undoubtedly the major context of kinship activity in Britain is provided by the household as a domestic group. It usually constitutes an important base from which the individual operates in the wider society. Major provision for the basic physical needs such as food, drink, and shelter, and for procreation is commonly made within its confines. The household has no monopoly of these functions, but it is certainly the dominant agency which caters for them. Household composition is closely related to the growth, development and decline of nuclear family units, and it is most instructive to examine both intra-household and inter-household linkages in relation to the operation of kinship principles.

These conceptualisations of the principles of kinship and of the development cycle of the domestic group, however, are at a high level of generality, and it is extremely important to bear in mind that the conceptual framework presented is only a guide for analysis. Empirical studies clearly demonstrate that the general principles and basic structure must be flexible enough to permit interpretation of very different patterns and sequences of social action. Finally a general *caveat* is perhaps in order. It is surprising how little information upon family and kinship in Britain has been collected *systematically*. The data presented as evidence in this text have been sifted from information currently available, but they cover only a relatively small proportion of the evidence which a sociologist would ideally wish to consider. It is only to be expected, therefore, that future research will both contribute to the construction of improved theoretical models and provide a sounder empirical base.

Appendix

British kinship terminology and kinship classifications

These diagrammatic representations of kin linkages and kin groupings are intended to supplement the text of Chapter 2. The following conventions have been adopted.

Ego is either male or female: the relationships traced in each diagram are those between ego and various categories of kin. (Distinctions are made according to sex except in the case of ego and ego's spouse.)

The usual formal kinship term applied to a particular category of kin in the British kinship system is used. (But 'spouse' is used throughout instead of husband or wife.)

Exact genealogical relationships are indicated in brackets alongside the normal kin term.

The following abbreviations are used to indicate exact genealogical relationships with ego:

Mo = mother
Fa = father
Br = brother
Si = sister
So = son
Da = daughter
Sp = spouse (either sex)

These abbreviations when used in combination indicate the way in which any particular relationship is traced: thus MoBrSo means mother's brother's son/s—the ordering of the abbreviation indicates the way in which the relationship is traced from ego outwards.

Marriage is denoted by $=$.

Ties in the direct line of descent are denoted by vertical lines. Horizontal lines in combination with vertical lines indicate that the same type of direct kin tie applies to two or more persons, (e.g. ⌐‾‾‾‾⌐).

Seven diagrams are used to distinguish egos:

I Family of Origin, II Family of Marriage, III First Degree Kindred, IV First Degree Affines, V Second Degree Kindred, VI Second Degree Direct Affines, and VII Second Degree Indirect Affines.

I FAMILY OF ORIGIN.

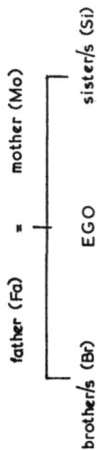

```
            father (Fa)    =    mother (Mo)    sister/s (Si)

                                EGO
        brother/s (Br)
```

II FAMILY OF MARRIAGE.

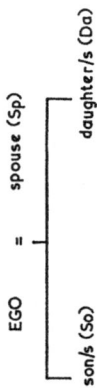

```
                        EGO    =    spouse (Sp)    daughter/s (Da)

        son/s (So)
```

III FIRST DEGREE KINDRED.

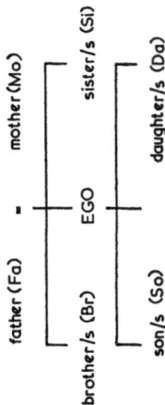

```
            father (Fa)    =    mother (Mo)    sister/s (Si)

                                EGO            daughter/s (Da)
        brother/s (Br)
        son/s (So)
```

IV FIRST DEGREE AFFINES.

```
                        father-in-law (SpFa)    =    mother-in-law (SpMo)    sister/s-in-law (SpSi)

                                                EGO=spouse (Sp)
        brother/s-in-law (SpBr)
```

V SECOND DEGREE KINDRED.

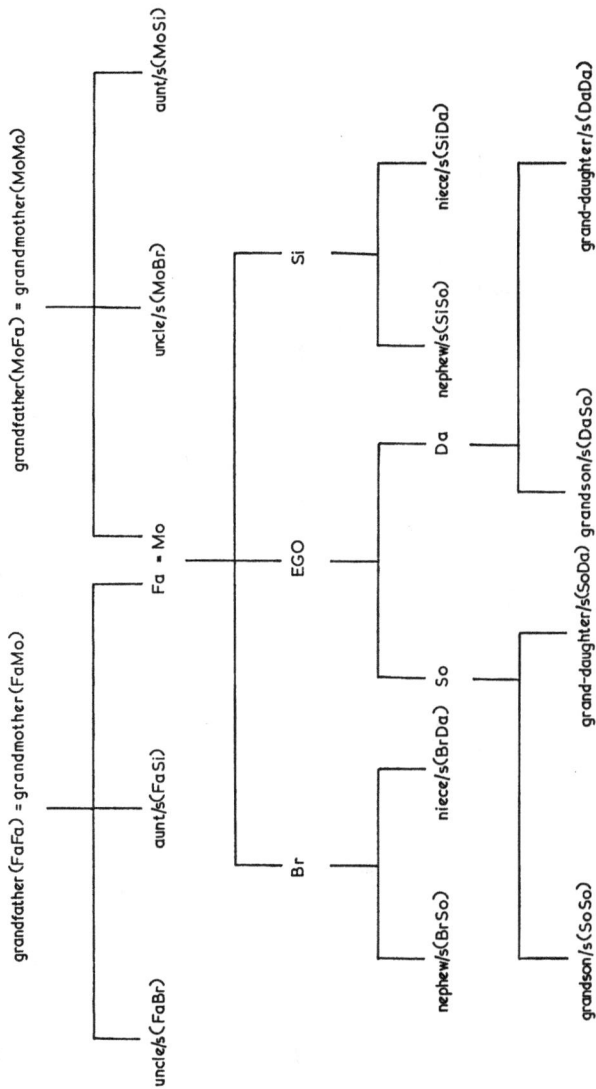

VI SECOND DEGREE DIRECT AFFINES.

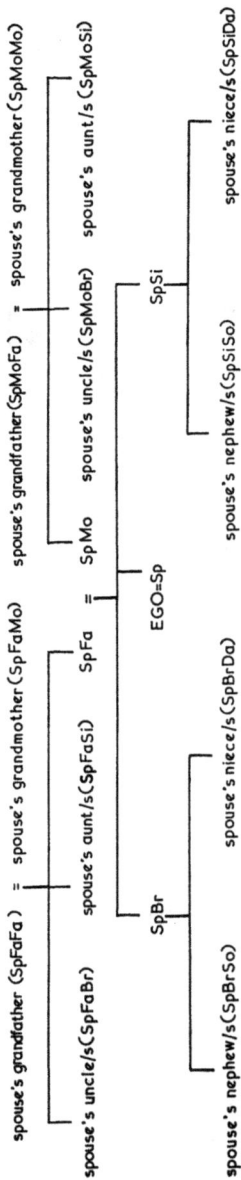

spouse's grandfather (SpFaFa) = spouse's grandmother (SpFaMo)   spouse's grandfather (SpMoFa) = spouse's grandmother (SpMoMo)

spouse's uncle/s (SpFaBr)   spouse's aunt/s (SpFaSi)   SpFa = EGO=Sp   SpMo   spouse's uncle/s (SpMoBr)   spouse's aunt/s (SpMoSi)

spouse's niece/s (SpFaBrDa)   SpBr   spouse's niece/s (SpBrDa)   spouse's nephew/s (SpSiSo)   SpSi   spouse's niece/s (SpSiDa)

spouse's nephew/s (SpFaBrSo)   spouse's nephew/s (SpBrSo)

VII SECOND DEGREE INDIRECT AFFINES.

Fa=Mo   SpFa=SpMo

Br = sister/s-in-law (BrSp)   Si=brother/s-in-law (SiSp)   EGO = Sp   SpBr=sister/s-in-law (SpBrSp)   SpSi=brother/s-in-law (SpSiSp)

N.B. In the case of spouse's sister-in-law and spouse's brother-in-law the terminology is 'merged' to sister-in-law and brother-in-law.

Suggestions for further reading

Works on the British kinship system

ROSSER, C., and HARRIS, C. C., *The Family and Social Change*, 1965, London: Routledge and Kegan Paul. This is an excellent research report on the immediate kin relationships of approximately 2,000 randomly selected families in the County Borough of Swansea.

FIRTH, R., *Two Studies of Kinship in London*, 1956, L. S. E. Monographs on Social Anthropology No. 5, London: Athlone Press. This contains a masterly introduction to the study of the British kinship system, followed by two case studies.

BOTT, E., *Family and Social Network*, 1957, London: Tavistock Publications. This is an exploratory study of the social networks and conjugal roles of twenty married couples in London, which has had a considerable influence on subsequent writings on marriage in both Britain and the U.S.A.

YOUNG, M., and WILLMOTT, P., *Family and Kinship in East London*, 1957, London: Routledge and Kegan Paul. This was the first research report published by the Institute of Community Studies. It contains a wealth of information on certain aspects of family life in Bethnal Green.

WILLIAMS, W. M., *A West Country Village Ashworthy*, 1963, London: Routledge and Kegan Paul. This research report is based upon research carried out in a rural community and concentrates on the three topics of family, kinship, and land.

General works and readers useful for comparative studies

GOODY, J., ed., *The Developmental Cycle in Domestic Groups*, 1958, Cambridge Papers in Social Anthropology No. 1, London: Cambridge University Press.

SCHNEIDER, D. M., and GOUGH, K., *Matrilineal Kinship*, 1961, Berkeley: University of California Press.

RADCLIFFE-BROWN, A. R., and FORDE, D., eds., *African Systems of Kinship and Marriage*, London: Oxford University Press.

GOODE, W. J., *World Revolution and Family Patterns*, 1963, New York: Free Press of Glencoe.

CHRISTENSEN, H. T., ed., *Handbook of Marriage and the Family*, 1964, New York: Rand McNally.

Bibliography

ARENSBERG, C. M., and KIMBALL, S. T. (1940) *Family and Community in Ireland*, New Haven: Harvard University Press

BERENT, J. (1954) 'Social Mobility and Marriage: A Study of Trends in England and Wales', in Glass, D. V. ed., *Social Mobility in Britain*, London: Routledge and Kegan Paul

BERNSTEIN, B. (1958) 'Some Sociological Determinants of Perception', *British Journal of Sociology*, 9, 1958, 159-174

BERNSTEIN, B. (1959) 'A Public Language', *British Journal of Sociology*, 10, 1959, 311-326

BOOTH, C. (1902) *Life and Labour of People of London*, vols. 1-17, London: Macmillan

BOTT, E. (1957) *Family and Social Network*, London: Tavistock Publications

BURGESS, T. (1964) *A Guide to English Schools*, London: Penguin Books

CHAPMAN, D. (1955) *Home and Social Status*, London: Routledge and Kegan Paul

CHESSER, E. (1956) *The Sexual Marital and Family Relationships of the English Woman*, London: Hutchinson

CHRISTENSEN, H. T. (1964) *Handbook of Marriage and the Family*, New York: Rand McNally

CROZIER, D. (1965) 'Kinship and Occupational Succession', *Sociological Review*, 13, 1965, 15-43

DENNIS, N., HENRIQUES, F., and SLAUGHTER, C. (1956) *Coal is Our Life*, London: Eyre and Spottiswoode

DOUGLAS, J. W. B. (1964) *The Home and the School*, London: Mac-Gibbon and Kee

ELIAS, N., and SCOTSON, J. L. (1965) *The Established and the Outsiders*, London: Frank Cass & Co

EVANS-PRITCHARD, E. E. (1961) *Kinship and Marriage among the Nuer*, London: Oxford University Press

FIRTH, R. (1956) *Two Studies of Kinship in London*, L.S.E. Monographs on Social Anthropology No. 5, London: Athlone Press

FIRTH, R. (1964) 'Family and Kinship in Industrial Society', *Sociological Review Monograph* No. 8, 1964, 65-87

FLOUD, J. E., HALSEY, A. H., and MARTIN, F. M. (1957) *Social Class and Educational Opportunity*, London: Heinemann

FRANKENBERG, R. (1957) *Village on the Border*, London: Cohen and West

FRAZER, E. (1959) *Home Environment and the School*, University of London Press

GLASS, D. V., ed. (1954) *Social Mobility in Britain*, London: Routledge and Kegan Paul

GOLDTHORPE, J. H., and LOCKWOOD, D. (1963) 'Affluence and the British Class Structure', *Sociological Review*, 11, 1963, 133-163

GOODE, W. J. (1956) *After Divorce*, New York: Free Press of Glencoe

GOODE, W. J. (1959) 'The Theoretical Importance of Love', *American Sociological Review*, 24, 1959, 38-47

GOODE, W. J. (1963) *World Revolution and Family Patterns*, New York: Free Press of Glencoe

GOODE, W. J. (1964) 'Family Disorganization', in Merton, R. K., and Nisbet, R. A., *Contemporary Social Problems*, 1964, London: Rupert Hart-Davis

GOODY, J., ed. (1958) *The Developmental Cycle in Domestic Groups* 1958, Cambridge Papers in Social Anthropology, No. 1, London: Cambridge University Press

GORER, G. (1955) *Exploring English Character*, London: Cresset Press

GRINDER, R. E. (1963) *Studies in Adolescence*, London: Macmillan

GUTTSMAN, W. L. (1963) *The British Political Elite*, London: MacGibbon and Kee

HARTLEY, S. M. (1966) 'The Amazing Rise of Illegitimacy in Great Britain', *Social Problems*, 44, 1966, 533-545

HUBERT, J. (1965) 'Kinship and Geographical Mobility in a Sample from a London Middle-Class Area', *International Journal of Comparative Sociology*, 6, 1965, 61-80

KERCKHOFF, A. C., and DAVIS, K. E. (1962) 'Value Consensus and Need Complementarity in a Mate Selection', *American Sociological Review*, 27, 1962, 295-303

KLEIN, J. (1965) *Samples from English Cultures*, vols. 1-2, Routledge and Kegan Paul

LUPTON, T., and WILSON, C. S. (1959) 'The Social Background and

Connections of Top Decision Makers', *Manchester School*, 27, 1959, 30-51

MALINOWSKI, B. (1932) *The Sexual Life of Savages*, London: Routledge and Kegan Paul

MARRIS, P. (1958) *Widows and their Families*, London: Routledge and Kegan Paul

MAYHEW, H. (1851) *London Labour and the Poor*, vols. 1-2, London: George Woodfall and Son

MITCHELL, G. D., LUPTON, T., HODGES, M. W., and SMITH, C. A. (1954) *Neighbourhood and Community*, Liverpool University Press

MOGEY, J. M. (1947) *Rural Life in Northern Ireland*, London: Oxford University Press

MOGEY, J. M. (1956) *Family and Neighbourhood*, London: Oxford University Press

NEWSON, J., and NEWSON, E. (1963) *Infant Care in an Urban Community*, London: Allen and Unwin

PARSONS, T. (1951) *The Social System*, New York: Free Press of Glencoe

PARSONS, T. (1954) *Essays in Sociological Theory* (rev. ed.), New York: Free Press of Glencoe

RADCLIFFE-BROWN, A. R., and FORDE, D., eds. (1950) *African Systems of Kinship and Marriage*, London: Oxford University Press

REES, A. D. (1950) *Life in a Welsh Countryside*, Cardiff: University of Wales Press

REGISTRAR GENERAL (1962) *Census 1951 Great Britain One Per Cent Sample Tables*, part II, London: H.M.S.O.

REGISTRAR GENERAL (1964a) *Census of England and Wales 1961 Housing Tables*, part I, London: H.M.S.O.

REGISTRAR GENERAL (1964b) *The Registrar General's Statistical Review of England and Wales*, 1962, part II, London: H.M.S.O.

REGISTRAR GENERAL (1965) *The Registrar General's Statistical Review of England and Wales*, 1962, part III, London: H.M.S.O.

REGISTRAR GENERAL (1966) *The Registrar General's Statistical Review of England and Wales*, 1964, part II, London: H.M.S.O.

REISS, I. R. (1960) *Premarital Sexual Standards in America*, New York: Free Press of Glencoe

RIVERS, W. R. H. (1906) *The Todas*, London: Macmillan

ROSSER, C., and HARRIS, C. C. (1961) 'Relationships through Marriage in a Welsh Urban Area', *Sociological Review*, 9, 1961, 293-321.

ROSSER, C., and HARRIS, C. C. (1965) *The Family and Social Change*, Routledge and Kegan Paul

SCHOFIELD, M. (1965) *The Sexual Behaviour of Young People*, London: Longmans, Green

BIBLIOGRAPHY

SCHNEIDER, D. M., and GOUGH, K. (1961) *Matrilineal Kinship*, Berkeley: University of California Press

SLATER, E., and WOODSIDE, M. (1951) *Patterns of Marriage*, London: Cassell

SPINLEY, B. (1953) *The Deprived and the Privileged*, London: Routledge and Kegan Paul

STACEY, M. (1961) *Tradition and Change a Study of Banbury*, London: Oxford University Press

TOWNSEND, P. (1957) *Family Life of Old People*, London: Routledge and Kegan Paul

TOWNSEND, P. (1962) *The Last Refuge*, London: Routledge and Kegan Paul

TOWNSEND, P. (1963) *Family Life of Old People* (rev. ed.), London: Penguin Books

TURNER, C. (1967) 'Conjugal Roles and Social Networks: A Reexamination of an Hypothesis', *Human Relations*, 20, 1967, 121-130

WILLIAMS, W. M. (1956) *The Sociology of an English Village; Gosforth*, London: Routledge and Kegan Paul

WILLIAMS, W. M. (1963) *A West Country Village: Ashworthy*, London: Routledge and Kegan Paul

WILLMOTT, P. (1963) *Evolution of a Community*, London: Routledge and Kegan Paul

WILLMOTT, P., and YOUNG, M. (1960) *Family and Class in A London Suburb*, London: Routledge and Kegan Paul

WIMPERIS, V. (1960) *The Unmarried Mother and her Child*, London: Allen and Unwin

YOUNG, M., and WILLMOTT, P. (1957) *Family and Kinship in East London*, London: Routledge and Kegan Paul

For Product Safety Concerns and Information please contact our EU
representative GPSR@taylorandfrancis.com
Taylor & Francis Verlag GmbH, Kaufingerstraße 24, 80331 München, Germany